Transforming Reading Skills in Secondary School

Transforming Reading Skills in the Secondary School is a commonsense text designed to help practitioners working in a mainstream context. The book suggests ways to develop the underlying skills necessary for good reading through multiple pathways such as mainstream subject lessons, individual and small group support sessions, whole school initiatives, the use of reading mentors and home–school liaison opportunities. Brimming with ideas and activities, Pat Guy explores a variety of different aspects of reading, including:

- how reading is taught and why it is such an important skill for the individual
- how to motivate the reluctant reader
- the role played by the mainstream and specialist teacher
- underlying problems pupils may face
- how to increase parental involvement
- reasons why a pupil's comprehension might be limited
- the role of the school librarian
- the relevance to reading of vocabulary and general knowledge.

Anyone wanting to develop the reading skills of secondary pupils who struggle will find this a resource they return to time and time again.

Pat Guy is an experienced teacher who has taught pupils with reading difficulties in mainstream schools for over twenty-five years.

nasen

Helping Everyone Achieve

nasen is a professional membership association that supports all those who work with or care for children and young people with special and additional educational needs. Members include teachers, teaching assistants, support workers, other educationalists, students and parents.

nasen supports its members through policy documents, journals, its magazine *Special!*, publications, professional development courses, regional networks and newsletters. Its website contains more current information such as responses to government consultations. **nasen**'s published documents are held in very high regard both in the UK and internationally.

Other titles published in association with the National Association for Special Educational Needs (nasen):

Language for Learning in the Secondary School
A practical guide for supporting students with speech, language and communication needs
Sue Hayden and Emma Jordan
2012/pb: 978-0-415-61975-2

Assessing Children with Specific Learning Difficulties
A teacher's practical guide
Gavin Reid, Gad Elbeheri and John Everatt
2012/pb: 978-0-415-67027-2

Using Playful Practice to Communicate with Special Children
Margaret Corke
2012/pb: 978-0-415-68767-6

The Equality Act for Educational Professionals
A simple guide to disability and inclusion in schools
Geraldine Hills
2012/pb: 978-0-415-68768-3

More Trouble with Maths
A teacher's complete guide to identifying and diagnosing mathematical difficulties
Steve Chinn
2012/pb: 978-0-415-67013-5

Dyslexia and Inclusion
Classroom approaches for assessment, teaching and learning, second edition
Gavin Reid
2012/pb: 978-0-415-60758-2

Provision Mapping
Improving outcomes in primary schools
Anne Massey
2012/pb: 978-0-415-53030-9

Promoting and Delivering School-to-School Support for Special Educational Needs
A practical guide for SENCOs
Rita Cheminais
2013/pb 978-0-415-63370-3

Time to Talk
Implementing outstanding practice in speech, language and communication
Jean Gross
2013/pb: 978-0-415-63334-5

Curricula for Teaching Children and Young People with Severe or Profound and Multiple Learning Difficulties
Practical strategies for educational professionals
Peter Imray and Viv Hinchcliffe
2013/pb: 978-0-415-83847-4

Successfully Managing ADHD
A handbook for SENCOs and teachers
Fintan O'Regan
2014/pb: 978-0-415-59770-8

Brilliant Ideas for Using ICT in the Inclusive Classroom, second edition
Sally McKeown and Angela McGlashon
2015/pb: 978-1-138-80902-4

Boosting Learning in the Primary Classroom
Occupational therapy strategies that really work with pupils
Sheilagh Blyth
2015/pb: 978-1-13-882678-6

Beating Bureaucracy in Special Educational Needs
Helping SENCOs maintain a work/life balance, third edition
Jean Gross
2015/pb: 978-1-138-89171-5

Transforming Reading Skills in the Secondary School
Simple strategies for improving literacy
Pat Guy
2015/pb: 978-1-138-89272-9

Developing Memory Skills in the Primary Classroom
A complete programme for all
Gill Davies
2015/pb: 978-1-138-89261-3

Transforming Reading Skills in the Secondary School

Simple strategies for improving literacy

Pat Guy

Routledge
Taylor & Francis Group
LONDON AND NEW YORK

First published 2015
by Routledge
2 Park Square, Milton Park, Abingdon, Oxon OX14 4RN

and by Routledge
711 Third Avenue, New York, NY 10017

Routledge is an imprint of the Taylor & Francis Group, an informa business

© 2015 P. Guy

The right of P. Guy to be identified as author of this work has been asserted by her in accordance with sections 77 and 78 of the Copyright, Designs and Patents Act 1988.

All rights reserved. No part of this book may be reprinted or reproduced or utilised in any form or by any electronic, mechanical, or other means, now known or hereafter invented, including photocopying and recording, or in any information storage or retrieval system, without permission in writing from the publishers.

Trademark notice: Product or corporate names may be trademarks or registered trademarks, and are used only for identification and explanation without intent to infringe.

British Library Cataloguing in Publication Data
A catalogue record for this book is available from the British Library

Library of Congress Cataloging in Publication Data
Guy, Pat.
Transforming reading skills in the secondary school: simple strategies for improving literacy / Pat Guy.
pages cm
1. Reading (Secondary) 2. Reading comprehension. 3. Literacy. I. Title.
LB1632.G88 2016
428.4071'2—dc23
2014046025

ISBN: 978-1-138-89270-5 (hbk)
ISBN: 978-1-138-89272-9 (pbk)
ISBN: 978-1-315-69542-6 (ebk)

Typeset in Sabon
by Book Now Ltd, London

Contents

PART I
Promoting reading in the secondary school   **1**

    Introduction   3

1 Overcoming barriers to reading development   4

    Undiagnosed medical problems   4
    Limited language skills   6
    A restricted vocabulary   7
    A poor general knowledge   11
    Issues with attention   11
    Assumed developmental delay   12
    A specific learning style   13
    Limitations of memory   14

2 Effective support in withdrawal lessons   17

    Student reading questionnaires   18
    Reading mentors   19
    Training reading volunteers/mentors from the local community   20
    Appropriate approaches the mentors should take   21
    Suitable resources for use with secondary readers   22
    How to encourage and prompt readers   24
    Developing the student's comprehension   26

3 Improving reading through mainstream lessons   29

    Ensuring the readability of subject texts matches student's reading age   29
    Supporting students' reading of non-fiction reading material   31
    Developing comprehension   33
    Different ways to support reading comprehension   35
    Extending understanding of subject vocabulary   40
    Increasing student reading speed   42

4 Whole school reading events   45

    Increasing student motivation   45
    Holding reading events   48
    Strengthening home–school links   49

Raising the profile of the school library 51
Promoting reading in the form room 53
Organising whole school initiatives 54

5 Stand alone reading lessons   55

Lesson 1: Reading habits and reading techniques 55
Lesson 2: Generic vocabulary 58
Lesson 3: General knowledge 63
Lesson 4: Reading speed 65
Lesson 5: Reading comprehension 67
Lesson 6: Subject-specific vocabulary 69

PART II
Practical exercises, advice sheets and hand-outs to support staff, parents, carers and students   73

6 Advice Sheets   75

Advice Sheet 1: Advice for parents – hearing your child read 76
Advice Sheet 2: Advice for parents – reading with your child 78
Advice Sheet 3: Advice for parents – suggestions for suitable reading resources 79
Advice Sheet 4: Assessment of vocabulary and general knowledge 80
Advice Sheet 5: Developing active reading – advice for mainstream teachers 81
Advice Sheet 6: Games and activities to support the development of subject vocabulary 82
Advice Sheet 7: Generic reading comprehension exercises for PHSE and study skills lessons 87
Advice Sheet 8: Promoting reading in the form room 88
Advice Sheet 9: Resources to support students' reading in withdrawal lessons 89
Advice Sheet 10: Slow reading: why it happens and how to help individual readers 92
Advice Sheet 11: Student advice sheet – how to improve your comprehension 94
Advice Sheet 12: Using newspapers as a reading resource 95

Glossary   96
References and resources   98
Index   99

Part I

Promoting reading in the secondary school

Introduction

I have been involved in the teaching of reading for over thirty years, initially as a primary school teacher, then as an LEA (Local Education Authority) Advisory Teacher working with pupils with literacy difficulties and, for the last fifteen years, as a SENCo (Special Education Needs Co-ordinator) in secondary schools. Over this period of time I have become aware of the performance of a large group of pupils who chose not to read and of the implications that this has for their final level of academic achievement. These students are able to decode adequately, but find comprehension increasingly difficult as they move through secondary school. Their problems remain unidentified as an individual's reading comprehension is assumed to be at the level of their decoding ability.

Many books explore the support needed by pupils with specific reading weaknesses, but few investigate the difficulties faced by these students whose reading skills stall at secondary school. *Transforming Reading Skills in Secondary Schools* identifies some of the less obvious, but common, barriers to achievement: limitations of general knowledge, a restricted vocabulary, low motivation, a weak memory and narrow reading experience, all of which limit pupil performance and, unbeknown to the adults working with them, create obstacles to their achievement. Support may be targeted erroneously towards the end result of the knowledge gap and resources and effort wasted: putting strategies into place to help a student with concentration problems will not be effective when the student lacks concentration because of poor comprehension.

Transforming Reading Skills in Secondary Schools is a commonsense publication designed to help the practitioner working in the mainstream context. The book suggests ways to develop the underlying skills necessary for good reading through multiple pathways: mainstream subject lessons, individual and small group support sessions, whole school initiatives, PHSE (Personal Health and Social Education) lessons, library events, the use of reading mentors and home–school liaison opportunities.

All support strategies and advice sheets are clearly presented and can be easily incorporated into lessons without the need for major adjustments to planning. Input of a steady 'little and often' nature from all adults involved with the students will have a positive effect on pupils' reading, improving their performance across the curriculum.

There is a clear and established correlation between poor literacy, low pay, poor qualifications and unemployment and reading is an easy, cost-effective way to improve the life chances of those students who do not have opportunities for real-life experiences such as travel, cultural visits and events, or regular exposure to formal language. If we are able to persuade pupils to read, help to raise their level of skill to make reading as easy as possible and provide entertaining and purposeful reading activities, we will be able to improve their overall performance and remove this invisible barrier to their learning.

Chapter 1

Overcoming barriers to reading development

How to help students who have:

- undiagnosed medical problems: hearing loss; visual difficulties
- limited language
- a restricted vocabulary
- a poor general knowledge
- issues with attention
- assumed developmental delay
- a specific learning style
- limitations of memory: visual memory; auditory memory difficulties.

Undiagnosed medical problems

As a first step, it is important to rule out the possibility of any underlying physical problems. It is easy to assume a student has some sort of specific reading difficulty, when they are actually experiencing a medical difficulty.

A degree of hearing loss

Might the student have an undetected hearing problem? Some students will have an intermittent hearing loss, the most common of these being glue ear. Glue ear occurs when the individual has frequent colds or a runny nose, the middle ear fills with fluid and the student's hearing is limited. Any sort of deficiency in hearing will affect reading ability. In the early stages of reading, it would be easy to think a child with an undiagnosed hearing problem had a specific learning difficulty, for example, when they are unable to hear the difference between the letters 'b', 'd', and 'p' because the letters sound the same when you have the equivalent of a permanent heavy cold. When an older student does not quite hear the correct pronunciation of words, they will have little idea of how to say the words when reading aloud.

Students may be unaware of their problem and, as the hearing loss is intermittent, it might not be picked up by the usual screening checks.

Typical behaviour of an individual with a hearing difficulty would include: straining forward to hear what is being said, watching the speaker's lips closely, regularly asking for information to be repeated, an apparent lack of attention, ear-ache, tiredness, indistinct speech, poor pronunciation or monotonous speech patterns. The reading comprehension of students with hearing problems is likely to be patchy because of the unreliability of information input; some explanations will be heard and others will not.

> ### Support strategies for students with hearing loss
>
> - Send the child for an ENT (ear, nose and throat) assessment to gauge the severity and/or regularity of the loss.
> - Take extra time to ensure the student has understood what has been read. The student with a hearing problem is certain to have fragmentary general knowledge and understanding.
> - Spend some time directly clarifying the correct pronunciation of subject vocabulary, adding visual clues whenever possible.
> - When reading from a textbook, stand close to the student, read as clearly as possible with hands and book away from the mouth to enable the student to support their hearing by lip reading.
> - Try to reduce the amount of background noise when reading aloud. It can be difficult for students with a hearing problem to ignore some sounds and focus on others, as all sounds will be heard at the same level.

Undiagnosed visual problems

Could the reader have some sort of undiagnosed visual difficulty? When reading, these individuals may tilt their head, rub their eyes, shut one eye, frown, squint, blink, rest their head on their arms to look at the page sideways or hold the book too close or too far from their face. They may have problems identifying the correct order of letters within words, reading words in the correct order across the page, or omit words and omit or re-read lines.

The students may not be aware that others do not see print as they do. If every image they see is blurred or moving, they may assume this to be normal.

> To read successfully, students need a range of visual skills in addition to adequate sight.

Students must be able to coordinate their eye movements and focus both eyes on the same part of a word, follow a line of print without losing their place, maintain clear focus whilst reading, make quick focusing changes when reading from a book or board and then back to their notes, in addition to being able to process what they are seeing. If children have problems with any of these aspects of vision, they will experience difficulty with reading.

> ### Support strategies for students with visual problems
>
> If the student exhibits any of the signs of visual problems as described above, ask them about any difficulties they may experience. Is their vision sometimes clear and sometimes blurred? Do letters appear to be doubled or lines of words overlapping? If so, when does it happen and what do they do? Do they ever get dizzy or feel sick when they are reading? Do they get headaches when reading for long periods?
>
> - The more severe cases will need an assessment from an optometrist. An optometrist will diagnose less obvious visual problems such as tracking or accommodation weaknesses. Students may be prescribed corrective lenses or given eye exercise programmes.
> - Some students might find the glare of black print on white paper hard to tolerate or complain that the print moves on the page. Sometimes mild problems can be alleviated by using coloured A4 plastic sheets as overlays. Worksheets copied onto pastel coloured paper rather than white also seem helpful, with dark grey rather than black print helping to reduce contrast.
>
> *(Continued)*

(Continued)

- Older copies of books with faded or creamy coloured paper are easier for some students to read because the contrast between print and paper is reduced.
- When students are reading from the computer screen or whiteboard, the colour of the background can be changed and font size enlarged.
- Position students who you suspect experience visual problems close to the board, under adequate lighting and away from reflective surfaces to ensure reading is as easy as possible.
- Ruler-sized strips cut from coloured A4 plastic sheets can be used as a combined reading guide and overlay. This will make it easier for students to keep their place on the page in addition to reducing glare.
- Keep sets of A4 magnifying sheets for students to borrow.
- Coloured rather than black pens for whiteboards can help to minimise visual stress.

Worksheets will require similar consideration:

- A plain font is preferable; students can have additional difficulties with the recognition of words printed in an ornate style.
- Print needs to be of an adequate size and at least a 12 point.
- Do not use capitals for whole words as the words will all appear to be of the same size and shape. This will make it more difficult for the reader to recognise words quickly; telephone being a more recognisable shaped word than TELEPHONE.
- Unjustified text will help the reader to keep their place and read fluently. When the beginning of a word is on one line and the end of the word on another, it will be hard for some readers to read without stumbling.

Limited language skills

Any students experiencing underlying language problems will have difficulties with decoding. These will exist alongside the less obvious weaknesses in comprehension, vocabulary, the processing of text at speed and interpretation of formal text structure.

> At the age of 16 years, 49% of students who have a history of Speech, Language and Communication needs would be expected to experience problems with the accuracy of reading (decoding). However, 74% will experience difficulties with the comprehension of a text and this may be less immediately obvious than the difficulties associated with decoding.
>
> (Conti-Ramsden and Botting, 1999)
>
> A survey of two hundred young people in an inner city secondary school found that 75% of them had speech, language and communication problems that hampered their learning.
>
> (Sage, 1998)

The importance of the part played by spoken language in reading development cannot be underestimated. Spoken language precedes reading and a child must be orally competent before developing reading skills. All individuals' language will develop at different rates and when a student's language is immature or underdeveloped, the effect this will have on their reading will need to be considered. Any student with limited language skills will be at an immediate disadvantage when reading secondary texts.

Problems that will affect a student's decoding will include:

- A limited appreciation of sounds and speech patterns. If individual words are pronounced sloppily – 'fing' for 'thing', 'free' for 'three' – letter/sound links will appear inconsistent and confusing. If words are run together in speech, for example, 'innit, wotsama'er, a pupil may be unaware of their separate nature in text.
- The student's auditory discrimination may not be refined enough to distinguish between sounds that differ in small ways such as 'though' and 'foe'.
- Some individuals find it difficult to recognise rhyme. Whilst not a major concern in itself, the ability to recognise rhyme forms part of the underlying set of skills that support reading. The ability to hear rhyme helps with decoding, for example, 'The word you are looking for begins with an "n" and sounds like: sight, fight and right'. If the reader knows the word 'down', then by association, they will be able to read the words: frowned, town, brown, gowns and drowning. Working on rhyme encourages the student to look at words analytically and to recognise groupings of letters within words: f/ield, sh/ield, y/ield and w/ield. This will help the weaker reader more than knowledge of letter sounds as it enables them to decode longer words.
- When words are misheard or misinterpreted, they may not be recognised in print: Les Stir for Leicester, SA for essay or Jim for Gym. Newspapers print student 'howlers' every year during the exam season and often, although the errors appear humorous, it is easy to understand the logical process the student has followed.

Speech and Language therapy services can appear to hold an ambivalent attitude towards older students, targeting their limited resources towards the younger child with more obvious speech difficulties. Few secondary teachers would appreciate the subtle language difficulties of secondary students and support services can seem uncertain of how to help.

Support strategies for students with underlying language problems

Students with an underlying problem with language will need precise and careful teaching.

- Whenever possible support information with additional visual input: films, photographs, diagrams, YouTube downloads, drawings or charts.
- Involve the student in practical and multi-sensory learning.
- Link new information to prior knowledge.
- Ensure students have adequate opportunities for discussion with their peers; other students are more likely to understand the reasons behind any misconceptions.
- Place students with problems carefully within groups so they are surrounded by good language role models.
- Never assume knowledge and be alert to confusions. Use activities such as DARTS, quick quizzes and mini-assessments to obtain regular feedback.
- Give practical examples of information that are linked to students' everyday experience.
- Encourage questions and give clear, precise answers, checking back to confirm student understanding.

A restricted vocabulary

Students with an underlying language problem, as described in the previous section, are certain to have a limited vocabulary. Other pupils may have a limited vocabulary and so appear to have underlying language issues. It can be difficult to separate these sorts of problems.

In secondary schools the complexity of the language and structure of written texts steadily increases. If a student has a limited vocabulary, there will be information in texts they can decode, but not understand. This problem will become part of a vicious circle as students with limited vocabulary will not be able to access texts that would extend their vocabulary. Educational research suggests that some groups of English students need the same sort of language development lessons offered to EAL (English as an Additional Language) students in order to access the curriculum successfully.

The gulf that steadily develops between different groups in terms of children's vocabulary is well documented:

- Children learn on average 2.2 to 2.4 new words each day between the ages of one and twelve years.
- By the age of four, children from higher socio-economic groups have been exposed to 45 million words and children from lower socio-economic groups, 13 million words. This gap will increase throughout childhood. 'To those that have, shall be given more', i.e. 'The Matthew Effect'.
- By Year 3 some pupils will have a vocabulary of 7,000 words and others 3,000.
- There is a direct correlation between the size of a student's vocabulary and their academic success.
- Students will need a vocabulary of 9,000 words to cope effectively with the secondary curriculum.
- 18-year-olds in full-time higher education will have a vocabulary of between 12,000 and 18,000 words.
- The majority of university graduates have a vocabulary of between 18,000 and 24,000 words.
- 25 per cent of the adult population have a vocabulary of between 6,000 and 12,000 words.
- There is a high correlation between levels of skills in speaking, listening, reading and writing.

> Working on vocabulary development in schools will raise reading achievement for all and help to narrow the gap between different social groups.

Reasons why some children's vocabulary levels may be low include:

- The use of TV for child minding and entertainment. When an adult talks or reads to a child, they are able to adjust their input to suit the child: explain, answer questions, ask questions, speed up or slow down the conversation, personalising the input to suit the child. A television programme has no way of knowing if the child is bored, frightened, disinterested, wants to know more or has left the room. For a child's vocabulary to increase, talk has to be interactive and not just heard by the child.
- Some households may be noisy; having continual background noise from television or radio that reduces opportunities for adult–child conversation.
- Verbal interaction with adults may be replaced by verbal interaction with other children in pre-school or nursery settings. Interaction between young children is certain to be limited in terms of modelling good speech patterns.
- Small family units may mean children have less contact with extended family and adult family friends who might have more time to talk with the children.
- Parents who have long travelling times and working hours may have little energy for conversations with their children in the evening. The same may apply to the child who has had an extended day at a nursery!
- Nannies and child minders may see their role as one of providing physical care rather than intellectual stimulation. Children's exposure to good language models may be reduced if their nannies or carers have a limited command of English themselves.
- There may be reduced teaching of rhymes and nursery songs within the modern family. Research shows that those children who know more nursery rhymes make better readers, probably as a result of their early exposure to rhyme, word play and the repetition of sounds.
- The pressure of the National Curriculum hurries some children into reading and writing before their oral language skills are adequately developed. An increase in the content of the

curriculum has meant less time is spent in the KS1 classroom listening to stories and looking at books.
- As a result of different working patterns, family meals and conversations around the dinner table may be a rarity.
- Solitary play activities such as computer games require limited verbal communication.
- Modern pushchairs face away from the adult and limit opportunities for child–adult conversation.
- A lack of understating among some parents about the importance of language and the connections between language and academic success.
- Some schools may pander to parental pressure and give young children homework, cutting back on the time the children could spend in reading for pleasure.

A limited vocabulary may be hidden by a student's apparent chattiness. Some students will appear to be articulate and confident, but may only use informal language. Informal, conversational speech is easy to understand. It is supplemented by clues the listener takes from facial expression and gesture, sentences tend to be short, often controlled by the amount of breath an individual can take with further conversation used for immediate clarification, such as, 'What do you mean?', 'Why do you say that?'. Although talkative students may have fluent speech, if their vocabulary is limited to conversational words, their ability to think in more abstract terms will be restricted. The more an individual reads, the more complex language they encounter and the wider their vocabulary will become. When a student develops an appropriate level of formal vocabulary, they will be able to keep pace with the more complex vocabulary of school texts, find it easier to maintain concentration, to follow arguments and to understand a range of material. If an individual has a poor vocabulary it will be easy to lose concentration in any situation where formal language is being used. Students would experience considerable difficulty following the language of *Great Expectations*, *The Tempest* or *Middlemarch* if their vocabulary was limited to conversational English. A challenging book may become inaccessible when the majority of the text is incomprehensible. When students find it difficult to follow class texts, they are likely to give up and lose concentration. Such students may be assumed erroneously to have a problem with attention.

When a student has an adequate vocabulary, their dependency on rote learning of isolated information will be reduced. Students with a poor vocabulary will try to learn by heart definitions for subject words and phrases that will be obvious to someone with a reasonable vocabulary, for example, 'Life expectancy = the average age in years a person can expect to live'.

As their language problem is unidentified, students will be at a loss to explain why they simply 'don't get it'. Sometimes another student can be the best person to explain word meanings, as they may have only just understood them themselves. Peers may be best able to explain vocabulary in words the student can understand.

Vocabulary needs to be taught both directly and indirectly, it is too important as a component of successful reading to be left to chance. It should be possible to introduce several new words and explain their meaning directly in every lesson. Students could be encouraged to record new words and definitions at the back of planners. Direct recording will emphasise the importance of vocabulary as part of subject knowledge.

New words enter the individual's vocabulary gradually. The stages of acquisition being:

1. The individual does not know the word.
2. The word is recognised, but cannot be defined.
3. The individual understands the word because of context or tone of voice. They will know they have heard the word, but will need to hear it in the context of a sentence before they are able to define it with an accurate shade of meaning.
4. The individual is able to use the word, understand the general and/or intended meaning, but cannot clearly explain it.
5. The individual is fluent with the word, both its use and definition.

On average a new word needs to be heard at least five times to get some idea of its meaning, ten times to be fully understood and fifteen times before the individual feels confident enough to use it themselves. However, while some individuals will acquire new vocabulary with ease, others will need additional assistance with learning.

Support strategies to develop vocabulary

- Encourage students to be curious about the meanings of words and to use paper and online dictionaries and thesauruses to look up word definitions.
- Small group discussions in class can help weaker students by exposing them to the slightly more advanced vocabulary of some of their peers. Other students who have only just grasped a concept may be able to explain it to their peers simply and in language they can understand.
- Create word maps for display on classroom walls giving alternatives for overused words. Use the posters for quizzes to ensure students read the words and do not view the lists as wallpaper. This sort of activity will present opportunities to point out shades of meaning as it is easy to miss nuance when vocabulary is unfamiliar. For example, the word 'cold' in 'I thought Gill was being rather *cold* towards me' being mistakenly replaced by 'I thought Gill was being rather bleak/wintery/chilly towards me'.
    - *nice* – enjoyable, agreeable, pleasant, good, fine, lovely, kind, amusing or wonderful
    - *walk* – glide, navigate, stomp, rush, stumble, tip-toe, sneak, march, slink, meander, wander or proceed
    - *beautiful* – lovely, attractive, good-looking, gorgeous, stunning, striking or handsome
    - *alone* – lonesome, abandoned, deserted, isolated, forlorn or solitary.
- Point out relationships between words. If the reader knows the meanings of the word 'expect', they can use that knowledge to work out the meaning of: expectation, expecting, expectant and expectancy. Raise students' awareness of prefixes and suffixes. 'Poly' meaning 'many' is a common prefix: polygamy in RE, polygon in Maths and polysyllabic in English. Students are more likely to remember these links if they are encouraged to work them out themselves. Here are some common prefixes and suffixes:
    - *circum* = around; for example: circumference, circumnavigate, circumspect
    - *post* = after; for example: postdate, postgraduate, postoperative, post-mortem, postnatal
    - *re* = again; for example: revision, returns, rearrange, replace, rewind
    - *un* = not; for example: unfriendly, unable, undone, unwilling, unresponsive
    - *-ess* = a female form; for example: lioness, duchess, baroness, heiress, actress, hostess
    - *-less* = without; for example: hopeless, guiltless, cordless, helpless, sleepless, harmless
    - *-gon* = cornered; for example: hexagon, polygon, octagon, pentagon.
- Discuss clues about words that students could take from the text. Sometimes a word is immediately followed by a clue about its meaning, for example, 'Nero was indecisive, he seemed unable to make up his mind'. This will give the opportunity to explain that in some complex sentences, the words are not always in an obvious order: 'The village, built as it was so close to the river, flooded on an annual basis.'
- Ask the students to collect synonyms and antonyms for words.
- Develop the students' curiosity. Encourage them to take an interest in the roots of the English language by drawing their attention to the origins of words. English has been influenced by many other languages as a result of: invasion (the Romans and Vikings); education (Latin and Greek); British colonisation (Indian and African words); immigration (Chinese and West Indian vocabulary); and international trade and global media (American words).
- Look at the origins of place names and surnames: Oxford, Bedford, Guildford, Stratford and Hungerford, Manchester, Dorchester, Rochester and Colchester.

A poor general knowledge

Any individual with a limited general knowledge will have reading comprehension problems. Without an adequate general knowledge even the simplest of texts will be rendered incomprehensible as readers will always interpret texts in the light of their existing background knowledge.

Even the most intelligent adult will be flummoxed by texts discussing unfamiliar topics. In this news report, an individual with some understanding of baseball would be able to make guesses at meaning, but an individual with no experience of the game would be lost.

> Machado sprained his right knee in the second inning while hitting a broken-bat grounder to shortstop. He was replaced by Gaynor, who came up in the fifth against Capuano (1–3) with a man on. Gaynor is quoted as saying, "I would've liked to have that pitch a little more down in the zone, probably expand it a bit, but I left it up and it caught too much of the plate".

If a student's general knowledge is limited, there will be occasions in school when texts make little sense. No matter how good your decoding is, if you are unfamiliar with the subject matter, your comprehension will be patchy. Many secondary school teachers will take a reasonable level of general knowledge for granted and assume a depth of subject knowledge that can be built on year after year. However, in reality, earlier misconceptions can often increase the likelihood of the development of further misconceptions.

Many students are unaware of what they don't know. Although it is possible to look up information on the internet, it can be difficult to know how to start when you have no knowledge of a topic. The more background knowledge an individual possesses, the easier it is to see the links between new information and existing understanding, One of the best ways to acquire background knowledge of topics is by reading widely.

See Advice Sheets 4, 5, 7, and 11 in Chapter 6.

Issues with attention

If students have low levels of attention, they are certain to experience difficulties with reading comprehension. Is the student able to maintain attention for a reasonable period of time? As a rule of thumb a student's concentration span will be approximately two minutes in excess of their chronological age, that is, the student of 14 years will be able to concentrate for 16 minutes. Inattention will present problems when students are reading or listening to others read. If they are not concentrating, they will be reading without any thought, unlikely to retain any information and so the task becomes pointless. A lack of attention may be linked to a language, hearing or visual deficiency.

> ### Support strategies for students with low levels of attention
>
> - Check the *reasons* for the student's poor attention, for example, do they have a problem with their hearing? Do they have adequate understanding of the language of the text? It would be difficult for anyone to maintain focus if they feel they are listening to gobbledegook.
> - Read material that is of interest to the pupil and at a level they can understand. Subject lessons can be enhanced by reading amusing, controversial or surprising snippets of information relevant to classroom topics from newspapers or magazines. There are numerous quality magazines that run articles of generic interest: *National Geographic*, *History Today*, *Scientific American* and *Billboard*. Articles from *Aquila* magazine are suitable for younger students. It can be hard to ascertain what specific pockets of general knowledge students do or do not possess and reading these sorts of short articles will have the additional advantage of promoting student discussion and supplementing an understanding of the world.
>
> *(Continued)*

> *(Continued)*
> - Make reading activities as interactive as possible. Ask the students to reproduce the information they have read or heard in an alternative format: diagram, poster, mind map, chart, flow diagram or comic strip. Active reading will support student focus and is a useful strategy for students to use when close reading with good comprehension is required.
> - Give groups of students articles to read and ask them to create questions relating to the text. They then read the text aloud as the rest of the class listen. When they have finished reading the passage, they ask the questions they have prepared and test their peers' levels of concentration. If a competitive element can be introduced, student motivation will be increased. Practising paying close attention in informal ways will increase students' awareness of how to focus and improve their ability to monitor their own levels of concentration in other situations.
> - Read a short passage aloud. Tell the students you will be asking them questions afterwards, so they are aware that they are expected to maintain focus and listen carefully. Allow students to take notes initially, and then move on to just listening.

Assumed developmental delay

The National Literacy Association advocates and campaigns for:

> A less prescriptive, more creative approach to reading and other aspects of literacy that recognises children learn in different ways and progress at different rates. Every child needs to experience the fun, pleasure and enjoyment of becoming literate.
>
> (www.nlaguide.co.uk/about)

If reading material is too difficult for an individual, they are likely to become disillusioned and feel they will never be able to read properly. It is important that reading texts are at an appropriate level for each reader.

There will be students whose level of development is always below that required at that particular moment. Students are all individual and will need different amounts of time to consolidate skills. Research shows that the development of the conductive material of neurons in the brain follows different patterns in different individuals and maturation of the areas required for reading is not fully completed until between five and seven years of age. To attempt to teach children to read before they are ready will be counter-productive.

> From the moment children in England enter the reception class, the pressure is on for them to learn to read, write and do formal written maths. In many schools, children are identified as "behind" with reading before they would even have started school in many other countries. There is no research evidence to support claims from government that "earlier is better".
>
> (Whitebread, 2014)

Some students will have been slow to start reading and see it as a difficult activity that they would prefer to avoid. They may not have been allowed adequate time to hone their skills to the required level. The student who has a summer birthday will have had a full year less in KS1 when the foundations for reading were being laid down. Some students will have started in the reception class just after their fourth birthday with children who were five already. The five-year-olds may appear to be acquiring reading skills at a faster rate and the younger children become disheartened. The situation would be similar to holding a running race for one- and two-year-olds: some children would still be crawling, others toddling and the rest running at very different speeds. It is essential that differences in developmental stages are taken into account in the classroom. Targeting provision at the average chronological age of a KS1 class may mean the reduction of motivation and self-confidence for significant numbers of children. Summer born students are at a particular disadvantage that is most obvious when they first enter school: 25 per cent of summer born pupils fail to reach expected levels at the end of Key Stage 1. This handicap does decline slowly over time, although age is still a factor in achievement levels at the end of KS4.

Other groups of students who may experience similar problems are those who have had prolonged periods of illness or hospitalisation and those whose school attendance record is poor. They may have gaps in their knowledge, be behind their peers and always playing catch up.

Although little can be done to ease the difficulties a child experiences when they are the youngest within their year or have had unavoidable periods of absence, teachers need to keep such factors in mind in order to develop pupils' reading at their own pace and maximise their confidence and interest levels.

A specific learning style

Not every method of teaching reading will suit every child. If students are unable to learn through one approach, another method or combination of methods will be necessary and should be put into place without question. In 2013, one in seven Year 6 children left primary school without having achieved the expected Level 4 in reading. These children will have been immersed for the previous six years in a phonic approach to reading, but it obviously has not been successful. They require a different approach and not more of the same.

How reading is taught

'Bottom-up' and 'Top-down' approaches to teaching reading refer to two fundamentally different teaching methods.

Bottom-up methods involve the teaching of synthetic phonics. Synthetic phonics is the teaching method that has been heavily promoted by the UK government in recent years. The approach involves building words up from their constituent parts, with phonemes (sounds) and graphemes (letters), being introduced before the students meet real words. All early reading material is linked to the graphemes that students have been taught. A strength of this method is that the reader is able to decode regularly spelt, unknown words. A criticism would be that the approach focuses on the decoding of text at the expense of meaning, with accuracy appearing to be more important than understanding or pleasure. There is a danger that pupils may feel they must read every word exactly as it appears on the page, decode each word from left to right, never guess a word as that would be cheating and show they were not applying the phonic rules that they had been taught. Decoding is presented as a puzzle where the reader studies the parts of each word, rather than understanding the meaning of the message.

> The development of students' reading is too important to be subject to political ideology.

Key aspects of the early stages of a synthetic phonics approach to reading are:

- Synthetic phonics focuses on the development of an awareness of letter sound–letter shape correspondence.
- Phonics are taught at the level of the individual phoneme from the outset.
- The phonemes (sounds) associated with the graphemes (letters) are taught at the rate of approximately six sounds per week.
- The sounds are taught in isolation and then blended together. Children might be taught a short vowel sound, for example 'i' at the same time as consonant sounds, 'p', 't' and 's'. Then the children are taught to make words with the sounds: tip, sip, sit and pit.
- Synthetic phonics involves the children rehearsing the writing of letter shapes alongside learning the letter–sound correspondences.
- Accuracy is considered all important. Reading speed, expression, and comprehension will come with time; the child's understanding of the relationship between the letters and the sounds is the first step.

Top-down methods are those used when students are taught to read with the focus being on the meaning of the text. Children are taught to recognise keywords with an emphasis on using context to guess words. Students begin to read graded books as soon as they can recognise a few keywords. Early books are built around the repetition of these keywords with other words gradually introduced. A strength of this system is that children are taught to recognise common words that are irregularly spelt, such as: was, their, said, does, they, father. A criticism of top-down methods is that students are taught little about how to break down unknown words.

The majority of children will be taught using a combination of the two methods, needing to be familiar with both approaches in order to be successful readers and ideally will be taught according to their response to the programme used. If a student had an auditory memory weakness, they might experience difficulty with a phonetic approach and benefit more from an approach that uses their visual skills, perhaps learning keywords by using flashcards. If they had slow processing ability, learning six sounds each week might not give enough consolidation and an approach involving repetition and over learning be more appropriate.

It would be impossible to stop a student from using a method they have worked out for themselves. Older students who have learnt to read through phonics are certain to use contextual clues to help them guess unfamiliar words. Students taught through 'look and say' recognition or whole word method will draw on their knowledge of alphabet sounds to separate an unfamiliar word into its constituent parts. It would be nonsensical to imagine individuals do not use a range of methods to help themselves. Whatever method is used, it is essential that the student experiences success. Reading is too important to allow a child think it is difficult: if one method isn't working, other approaches must be used.

> Different approaches to the teaching of reading are essential if individual students are to be supported effectively.

Limitations of memory

Students with **poor visual memories** will experience difficulties with the automatic recall of irregular words. Trying to remember words will put pressure on the students' short-term memory at a time when they need to retain information about overall content. Students will begin to read more complicated texts in secondary school with an increasing number of phonetically irregular words appearing in subject material. The occasional unfamiliar word will not affect fluency, but if several words in each sentence are not recognised and have to be decoded individually, overall meaning will be lost and reading become an unappealing chore.

Support strategies for students with limitations of visual memory

- Any student with poor visual recall for words will require additional exposure to subject vocabulary. Unknown subject or generic vocabulary could be identified and put onto a grid, such as the one below. The student reads these grids as often as possible and times themselves, the aim being to get faster and word recall to become automatic.

Erosion	condensation	evaporation	Cycle
Cycle	Evaporation	System	storage
Evaporation	System	storage	erosion
Erosion	Evaporation	condensation	cycle

Condensation	Cycle	Erosion	system
system	condensation	Cycle	evaporation

- Unknown keywords could be used for whiteboard games as part of the introduction or plenary of the lesson. Repetition of words will need to be an ongoing activity as if a student has a memory problem, learning ten new words each week does not mean the words will be remembered in the future.
- Computer programs offer vocabulary over learning, for example: the BBC Bitesize or Wordshark programs. Working on word recognition using IT gives opportunities for discreet repetition: students can practise reading and spelling words as often as desired without receiving any negative feedback.

Students with **poor auditory memories** will find it difficult to remember letter and sound links and the sequence of sounds in a word accurately. Their ability to decode polysyllabic words phonetically will be poor; they will have to remember the letter–sound correspondence correctly for several letters and then join the appropriate sounds together in the correct order. When reading aloud they will guess wildly, identifying words using minimal clues such as the grouping of similar letters, century becoming centre, cemetery, category or cutlery. All of their focus will be on decoding, so they may not recognise errors in sense: 'The previous cemetery had been one of revolution'.

When reading more complex texts, these readers will find it almost impossible to create any overall understanding of how parts of information fit together, all of their energy being focused on decoding as accurately as possible.

The students' spelling may reveal valuable information about their ability to remember the order of sounds in words: enonvirment for environment, Pissaco for Picasso or thernoneter for thermometer.

Support strategies for students with limitations of auditory memory

- Any remedial programme for secondary students will need to target the areas that are giving the student most problems. Targeting specific areas for focus will be seen as sensible by the student: they can improve their reading by concentrating on a few particular areas.
- Write words that confuse the student on blank cards and run through the sets or a few cards by way of an introduction or plenary to a lesson. The students could make their own sets of cards with words on one side and picture clues on the other.
- Students with auditory memory weaknesses will experience information overload; it will be hard for them to blend individual letters to make even quite small words. Encourage the student to focus on sections of words when decoding: recognising onset and rime will be easier than working with individual letters: n-ight, l-ight, r-ight, br-ight rather than s-l-i-g-h-t or m-i-g-h-t.
- Work on syllabification and breaking words down into smaller parts for sounding out. The specific place where a word is divided doesn't matter: mor/ning or morn/ing. The aim is for the student to recognise that the word is composed of constituent parts and that they should look for smaller parts within words: pro/tru/ding, em/ploy/ment, pop/u/la/tion and pre/scrip/tion. Compound words such as: desk/top, ex/port, web/site, work/bench, down/stream, home/work, in/let and sound/proof are good starting points for this sort of activity.

(Continued)

(Continued)

- When a student experiences sequencing problems, their reading of longer subject words will be littered with mispronunciations. These words will be pronounced in a variety of ways until the correct pronunciation is recognised. Unfamiliar words may not be recognised even when they have been accurately pronounced. Names can be particularly difficult to decode when the pronunciation seems illogical: Siobhan, Seamus and Niamh as opposed to Ben, Sam and Tom. This may present difficulties when reading aloud, for example, Joseph Buquet, Christine Daaé, Viscount Raoul de Chagny and Meg Giry from *The Phantom of the Opera*. The student will be aware of the need for fluency in front of an audience and be panicked into making wild guesses, so it is important that any unusual vocabulary is introduced and pronunciation clarified before reading to save any embarrassment. Students who have difficulty remembering sounds are certain to have difficulty remembering names, they will have problems as to who is who when following a text. This sort of difficulty can be helped by providing A4 sheets naming and giving brief notes about each character. The students can keep the sheets in the front of the subject folders.
- Send positive messages about confusions presenting opportunities for learning by having posters on the classroom wall with visual clues to support the pronunciation of more complex specialist vocabulary.
- Choral reading of texts, either as a class or in small groups within the class, will expose readers to the correct pronunciation of unfamiliar words. All levels of readers will mispronounce some of the words they have seen in reading material, but have never heard spoken aloud.
- Choral or shared reading will enable the student with a poor auditory memory to move some attention from decoding to remembering, providing more of an overview to support their comprehension.
- Auditory sequencing problems should not cause too many problems when reading silently unless a significant number of words cannot be decoded.

Chapter 2

Effective support in withdrawal lessons

This chapter discusses how to:

- use reading questionnaires and observation lists to target appropriate support
- assess readers' underlying skills: general knowledge, generic vocabulary and understanding of texts
- train reading mentors in the following: appropriate approaches to take when listening to readers; suitable resources for use with secondary students; how to encourage and prompt readers; ways to develop students' comprehension.

Hearing all students read would be good practice for all secondary schools to adopt and would benefit students of all abilities. Reading around the class in mainstream lessons cannot be a substitute for reading to an adult on a one-to-one basis. When all students have lessons, or part of lessons, set aside specifically for reading activities, they will be less likely to see additional reading practice as a form of punishment: negative attitudes can be reinforced when students have to miss breaks, lunch times or clubs to read.

> The most effective way to improve a student's reading is to hear them read.

The development of reading skills is of pertinence to *all* pupils: some will need additional practice to recall keywords, some will need extra help to understand advanced subject vocabulary, others to increase their reading speed or to be given suggestions to extend their range of reading material.

Readers can be divided into different groups at secondary and college level:

- Those students who read widely and continue to develop their reading.
- Competent readers who have stopped reading for pleasure. This could be for several reasons, perhaps as a result of the pressure of academic work or because they are unable to find interesting material. All of these students will have adequate ability, but may not be developing the level of skill necessary for further education, higher education and the world of work.
- Another group of readers will appear to be reading at an appropriate level, but have gaps in their skills. It is difficult to be certain whether students who can decode are also able to understand. Many students appear to read fluently, but decoding is the extent of their reading ability and they couldn't summarise or discuss what they have read. They may be uncertain about the meanings of individual words or more complex sentences. It is easy for this group to be overlooked by teaching staff who can overestimate their levels of understanding.
- Other readers will not have reached the level of competence necessary to read secondary level texts. Students will need to have a Level 4 in Key Stage 2 SATS in order to access the secondary curriculum and a significant number of students will not reach this standard.

As students move through secondary school and beyond, the gap between the reading levels of different individuals will increase. In any Year 7 intake, the range of reading ages may vary from that of a 7-year-old to a 17-year-old. This variance will be reflected across all of the sub-skills that underlie reading: speed of word recognition, knowledge of vocabulary, comprehension of text and so forth. Certain deficiencies will be more obvious to teaching staff than others and additional support is more likely to be offered to those students who are unable to decode, rather than to those with an underlying weakness with comprehension. When a student's comprehension levels are behind those of their peers and no support is offered, the gap between their reading level and that required by the curriculum will increase, their access to mainstream subjects be reduced and motivation impaired. The experience of a student with poor comprehension will be similar to that of an average ability student decoding a comparatively complex French text: they may be able to decode the words, but that will not guarantee an understanding of overall meaning. It is important that all of the students' reading skills are developed and not just their decoding ability.

Student reading questionnaires

When hearing readers, it may be useful to use a simple tick sheet to record their reading behaviour and level of skill. Observations made by the adult as the student reads will provide additional information about the type of support that would be most appropriate. More errors are likely to be made when students feel embarrassed or panicky so it is important for the reading mentor to appear relaxed and non-judgemental. The adult should not record every single error the student makes, but remember the student's two or three most regular errors, for example, missing out or re-reading lines, guessing at unfamiliar words or reversing words, so that 'on' becomes 'no', and then record the errors after the student has left to return to their class.

What sort of decoding errors are made? Look for any patterns of errors. Everyone will make mistakes when reading; it is the regular mistakes that need to be recorded, such as:

- Mispronunciations of phonetically irregular words that it could be assumed the reader would know: qu-A for quay or is-land for island.
- Substitutions: one word being substituted for a visually similar word: whipping for wiping or change for charge.
- A poor recall of keywords. The student does not appear to automatically recognise frequently used words such as: through, could, although, your, said and their.
- Reversals. This is when the word is read from right to left and not left to right: 'saw' for 'was' or 'on' for 'no'.
- When they come across unfamiliar words they have decoded on previous pages, do they behave as if the words had not been seen before?

What do students do when faced with an unknown word? Wait to be prompted? If they do this, they will need to be encouraged to use some of the strategies below. If they use only one of the strategies below, demonstrate use of the others. The aim of hearing the student read is to suggest ways in which they can help themselves to develop their independent reading skills.

- Try to sound the word out phonetically.
- Use syllables to break long words down into their constituent parts.
- Use context to make an informed guess.
- Use illustrations to make sensible guesses.
- Guess at the word using small parts as clues.
- Use a combination of approaches: context, phonics and matching the word to other known words that look similar.

Questions to ask the reader

Motivation

- Why do you think people read? What purpose does reading serve? Do they see reading as a purely school-based activity?
- Do you read for pleasure? If so, when and for how long?
- What sort of reading material do you enjoy?
- Do you prefer non-fiction to fiction or do you enjoy both?
- Who are your favourite authors? Why?
- What is your favourite book? Why?
- Do you ever read magazines or newspapers? If so, which ones?
- Does anything make reading hard for you? If so, what?
- Do you use the school and/or public library?
- What would you like to do when you grow up? How do you think reading is useful in that occupation?

Speed

- Do you feel that you read more slowly than your friends?
- Do you sometimes read so slowly that you find it hard to follow a story?

Comprehension

- Do you always understand everything you read?
- What do you do if you don't understand material? What sort of strategies do you use to help yourself?
- Could you summarise the plot of the book you are reading in English lessons at the moment?

Decoding confidence

- Do you enjoy reading aloud in class? If not, why?
- Do you sometimes find it hard to pronounce unfamiliar words?

Reading mentors

The Teaching and Learning Toolkit, published by the Sutton Trust and the Education Endowment Foundation in 2012, looked at the cost-effectiveness of resources used to support learning in schools. Peer tutoring emerged as one the most 'high impact/low cost' support strategies. Organising a system of peer mentors for reading provides benefits for all. The younger pupil is given extra opportunities to develop fluency, while the older student is provided with a chance to practise reading from lower level books, gaining confidence with material that may be close to their own reading age.

Reading aloud to mentors such as the Librarian, older students, volunteers from the community, students from local colleges, Learning Support staff and Teaching Assistants may seem less embarrassing than reading to teaching staff.

It is important to encourage parents and carers to read with and to their children for as long as possible. Send home regular Reading Newsletters with articles about the importance of

> Be aware that the parents of weak readers may be weak readers themselves.

reading, book lists, book reviews and information about the resources available in the Library. Keep a section of reading material in the library specifically for parents.

Training reading volunteers/mentors from the local community

Hold a few training sessions for volunteers covering basic approaches to tuition as well as the school's behaviour code, dress code, and fire and safety procedures. It is essential that volunteers are CRB (Criminal Record Bureau) checked and aware of child protection issues.

Some volunteers might welcome the opportunity to observe a lesson taken by a more experienced mentor or it may be possible to produce a short training DVD to cover the main points of reader mentoring for volunteers to take to watch at a time to suit them.

The training should be adapted according to the age and experience of the volunteer, but will need to cover the following:

1. The overall approach the mentors should take.
2. Suitable reading resources and where they can be found.
3. Approaches to be used to help students as they read.
4. How to prompt readers when they get stuck.
5. How to help the readers develop their comprehension.

Procedure for working with volunteer reading mentors

- Introduce all volunteers to the school librarian and give them a tour of the Library and/or the school's reading resources base.
- Share all sources of reading material, making suggestions of specific resources that individual readers might enjoy. Provide backup material for mentors to use for variety: card games, board games, word searches, crosswords and sets of blank cards to create Snap, Pelmanism and Bingo type activities.
- Organise a regular time for the volunteer to come into school to hear readers for as much or as little time as they are able to offer, expressing gratitude for all help given.
- Organise a suitable work area for the volunteer and have a backup plan in case this space is being used.
- Pre-select students to read. Have reserve lists for the occasions when individuals are absent or involved in other activities. Provide the volunteers with appropriate background information about the readers: their approximate reading age, any individual interests and subject strengths. The reluctant reader may have had previous negative experiences that have stopped them from reading for pleasure and they will need their confidence restored. One of the most important contributions a reading volunteer can make is to raise the individual's self-esteem, take an interest in them and their reading, focusing on what they can do rather than what they can't. This approach will include finding reading material that relates to the student's personal interests: books, magazines, websites, newspaper cuttings, booklets or leaflets linked to a career they may be interested in, a sport they enjoy, films they have seen, advice about keeping pets or background reading for exam subjects.
- Ensure that all staff working in the school's Reception or office knows the volunteers' names, when they will be in school and are available to help them whenever necessary.
- Discuss any student records to be kept and the organisation of liaison with the student's teacher, SENCo or adult within the school with responsibility for the reading volunteers. Recording systems will need to be simple and easily managed; perhaps a notebook or reading log kept on the Librarian's desk for students who read in the Library. Brief notes should be made after each session to record the amount read, the degree of student interest and engagement, any successful strategies used, particular words or word patterns that gave the reader problems in addition to any other general comments that could be used to inform future lessons.
- Remember to pass on the school's thanks to the volunteers on a regular basis.

Appropriate approaches the mentors should take

The following list sets out the overall approach that mentors should take when listening to readers.

- Allow time to get to know the students and their reading levels. Some students will be happy to read, others may be very anxious. It is important to maintain a relaxed approach when hearing reluctant readers.
- Encourage the reader to see regular reading practice as necessary for success. Sportsmen and women train, musicians put in hours of practice, dancers rehearse: the same principle applies to reading.
- Remember all students are different and there is no one perfect way to teach an individual to read: 'No single method or single combination of methods can successfully teach children to read' (The International Reading Association, 2000). No one will undermine a school's reading programme by using a commonsense approach. If adults display empathy towards students, perhaps explaining how they tackle words they don't recognise, students will feel reassured, as well as being able to extend the range of reading strategies they can use. Keep the approach light-hearted; if a student is able to work out the first part of a word phonetically, help them to guess the whole word using additional clues such as rhyme: 'The centre of an apple and rhymes with snore'. This will make decoding seem more like a game. Point out visual clues from illustrations and contextual clues from the sentence, paragraph or from the overall topic. Make reading fun, not a source of stress.

> Every strategy we use to teach reading is legitimate: there is no one magic formula.

- Be confident about using a pragmatic approach to hearing students read. If a story has several characters with names that the student is finding hard to remember, call them easier alternatives: Raoul Vicomte de Chagny becomes Roger and Armand Moncharmin, Arnie. This will ensure that the student's reading is as fluent as possible and they do not have to stop and stumble over unfamiliar names. Such things are not important in the bigger picture: the students should not be put off enjoying a story because the character's names are unusual. When it is essential to remember a name, work on the pronunciation using prompt sheets with simple sketches and 'sounds like' lists. When set texts have a large number of characters and students have difficulty remembering who is who, provide a crib sheet with a picture of the character and a little about their role in the text.
- Be flexible in your approach: if students appear tired, upset or overexcited, adapt the reading activity as would seem to be appropriate. If they are not focused enough to read, play games instead. How quickly can they recall keywords? Can they match subject words to definitions? Try word searches, crosswords, Pelmanism or Bingo.
- If it is essential to read around in the group, let students know in advance which section they will be reading to give them a chance to look ahead and work out any unfamiliar words. Divide the text into a number of lines if students are underconfident, perhaps everyone reads four lines and then it is the next person's turn. This will also ensure everyone remains engaged as turns to read will come round quickly. Agree within the group that no student corrects another person's errors as it is distracting to be interrupted. Allow the students to read in pairs if necessary to make the experience less daunting. Ensure reading material is at a level that guarantees reader success. Any negative peer response will make students feel under pressure to read as fluently as possible and to focus all their energy into decoding rather than understanding the text.
- Ask the student what they find or have found useful when trying to understand a text. Discuss whether they feel the strategy would be a good one to use in the future.

Suitable resources for use with secondary readers

This section gives guidance on suitable reading material, in general terms and also looks at non-fiction and fiction material.

- Give the student a choice of material: sometimes they will feel able to tackle something challenging and at other times, prefer to read easier text. A choice is reassuring as they will know they are not going to be constantly challenged, but can feel free to enjoy the lesson. Do not make the student feel they have to work from the beginning to the end of a book. It is perfectly reasonable only to read those sections of text that interest them.
- Drama and play scripts are excellent for reading aloud – readers can read in pairs or small groups. Weaker readers may feel more comfortable reading parts with limited, but regular, input. The process of acting out the story will assist in the understanding of the text. Reading and acting out sections of a class text or play in small groups will give students a chance to identify with the characters and action. Some students may be horrified at the idea of, not only being expected to read aloud, but also having to act, while others will relish the opportunity to be centre stage, so a discreet distribution of parts will be essential if everyone is to enjoy and benefit from the experience. However, as always, be prepared to be surprised; the student who enjoys reading in Drama may not be the student who likes to read in English lessons.
- Poetry is a subtle way to help students who continue to experience difficulty discriminating between sounds and recognising rhyme. Choral reading of short, rhythmic poems can be popular with less confident readers. Poems can be simple and humorous; their rhythm will help the student learn them by heart. Football chants, pop songs, riddles, limericks and raps will all assist with the development of an appreciation of rhythm and rhyme.
- Reading will develop in stages and to jump from simple to complicated texts will be too challenging for most students. Authors like Roald Dahl can bridge the gap and give the students experience of how the language of books develops.
- Do not be concerned if the student chooses easy books: they need to appreciate what it is like to read fluently.
- Reading song lyrics is a useful way to raise confidence. Students will be familiar with some lyrics and motivated to check the accuracy of their interpretations of specific tracks.
- IT can be popular with teenagers: text-to-speech software, e-books, blogs, kindles, iPods or CDs. Use specialist associations like 'Listening Books' for downloading or streaming books. Reading an e-book may seem more attractive than a paper version of the text and more in line with current methods of communication. Online newspapers and magazines, websites for sports teams and reviews for current films, concerts and television programmes will appear to be a more adult way of reading.
- Reading the subtitles from films and TV programmes, perhaps as a group or choral exercise, can provide amusing reading practice.

Non-fiction

Many students believe that reading fiction is the only form of 'proper' reading and might be happier reading information books. It is often assumed that one of the reasons that boys choose not to read is because the material presented in schools does not relate to their interests. However, many girls also find stereotypical fiction material unappealing and prefer information books. It is possible to find non-fiction material that relates to all possible areas of student interest: astronomy, sport, animals, film, cookery, travel, music, technology, art, politics, nature, cars, design, computers and fashion.

- Non-fiction material appeals to some readers because it can be presented in bite-sized pieces and dipped in and out of rather than having to be read sequentially.
- Atlases, brochures, encyclopaedias, instruction manuals and the internet all provide material that a reader can scan to find unusual, interesting articles.
- Biographies and autobiographies of famous sports, TV, film and music personalities can be popular, particularly when the student knows something about the individuals or is interested in their career.
- Magazines such as *National Geographic* have a wide selection of interesting material presented in short articles supported by good quality photographs and diagrams.
- If students enjoy gaming, they are certain to be interested in strategy guides.
- Trading cards give reading opportunities in the guise of a game.
- Newspapers can provide a source of accessible information. Students may watch the News on television and so have prior knowledge of the main articles. Sunday papers often give summaries of the events of a week, helping to develop students' knowledge of current affairs. They can be motivated to read more complex sections of the paper because of a personal interest, for example, in sport: the analysis of their football team's performance, mini biographies of players they admire, the politics behind an international competition or specialist training schedules.
- Comics and magazines provide interesting, bite-sized pieces of information. *Aquila*, junior sections of newspapers and editions of *National Geographic*, *BBC Music* and *BBC History* are all quality publications with text supported by interesting visual displays to capture a student's attention.
- Puzzle, quiz and joke books, for example the 'Where's Wally' series or The Usborne series of puzzle books will give purposeful reading practice.
- Try series of books using a 'If you liked this, you'll also enjoy ...' type of approach. Popular non-fiction series would include the Horrible History, Geography and Science books.
- Many board and card games require the players to read short pieces of text thereby involving students in indirect reading.

> Non-fiction has the additional advantage of improving the reader's general knowledge.

Fiction

- Sets of books can be popular. If a student reads and enjoys one book from a series, they might be encouraged to read others. Examples of this sort of material would be the Harry Potter, Twilight, the 'My Story' historical novels and the Animal Ark series.
- Certain genres of books (science fiction, fantasy, horror) will provide a wealth of potential reading material once the student's initial interest has been aroused. Examples of texts that could be used as 'ways in' would include: *An Unfortunate Series of Events* by Lemony Snicket, books from the *Star Trek* and *Star Wars* series, *Artemis Fowl* by Eoin Colfer, or *His Dark Materials* by Philip Pullman.
- Students may be attracted to the work of certain authors: Malorie Blackman, Harlan Coben, Roald Dahl, Anne Fine, James Patterson, Jacqueline Wilson or Enid Blyton. Lists of authors who write similar books can be obtained from bookshops, libraries and literacy associations in their, 'If you like this, you'll love this', sections.
- Read around topics to provide extension opportunities: *Carrie's War*, *Goodnight Mr Tom*, *The Machine Gunners*, *Anne Frank*, *The Silver Sword*, *I am David*, will all provide background information for the Second World War.
- The adult could read interesting extracts from the books or watch scenes from DVDs and films of classic texts – *Animal Farm*, *Pride and Prejudice*, *Wuthering Heights*, *Of Mice and Men*, *To Kill a Mocking Bird* – to whet the students' appetite.

- Theatre trips could be organised to see dramatic interpretations of fiction: *Matilda*, *The 39 Steps*, *Woman in Black*, *War Horse*, *Charlie and the Chocolate Factory*; or set plays such as: *Macbeth*, *Romeo and Juliet*, *The Crucible* and *The Tempest*. When students are able to see performances of plays, the text will come alive in a way that is impossible when reading from a book in the classroom.
- Comics, annuals and graphic novels can be motivating for some readers; words are minimal and pictures used to reinforce the main sequence of action filling any gaps left by reading limitations.
- Several book companies publish abridged versions of classics for emergent readers: *The Iron Man*, *The Secret Garden*, *Frankenstein*, *Wind in the Willows*, *Treasure Island*, *The Hound of the Baskervilles*, *Moby Dick*, *Five Children and It*, *The Railway Children* and *Tom's Midnight Garden*.
- Short stories can be more appealing to some students than a complete book. Paul Jennings, Conan Doyle's Sherlock Holmes series and Roald Dahl's short stories are all well written, entertaining and will interest teenager readers.
- EAL (English as an Additional Language) readers will provide suitably abridged versions of school set texts for the secondary age group.

How to encourage and prompt readers

As the student reads

- Depending on the student's age and ability level, read the first paragraph or page of the text to familiarise the student with the type of language being used and any topic vocabulary.
- Read parts of the text yourself to keep momentum going, a paragraph, a page or several pages depending on the student's fluency and motivation. Say that you will be doing this before starting the lesson or the student may think you hadn't realised how hopeless their reading was and that you are bored or feel sorry for them. If a reader is struggling, adapt the approach slightly to make the task easier; read the passage together or divide the text into paragraphs for both of you to read in turn. This will be better than abandoning an exercise and risk sending a negative message to the reader about their ability.
- When you read, whenever you make an error, correct yourself naturally and then move on to demonstrate to the student that making a few mistakes is nothing to be worried about.
- Model good reading. All students benefit from hearing good, entertaining readers. Such reading does not have to be over dramatic. Many weak readers think their reading is good when it has 'expression', preferably loud, whether the emphasis they are putting on words is correct or not. It is better to read clearly and at a natural level. Listening books and CDs are useful to demonstrate clear, entertaining reading. To demonstrate the subtle changes emphasis can make for meaning, read the sentences below stressing a different word each time the sentence is read and see if the students can register the differences.

    1. <u>Tina</u> did not say you wore her green jacket. (Someone else said it.)
    2. Tina <u>did</u> not say you wore her green jacket. (Strong indignant denial of saying it.)
    3. Tina did <u>not</u> say you wore her green jacket (Strong denial of saying it.)
    4. Tina did not <u>say</u> you wore her green jacket. (Tina implied it, but didn't say it.)
    5. Tina did not say <u>you</u> wore her green jacket. (Tina wasn't talking about you.)
    6. Tina did not say you <u>wore</u> her green jacket. (You did something else with it.)
    7. Tina did not say you wore <u>her</u> green jacket. (You wore someone else's.)
    8. Tina did not say you wore her <u>green</u> jacket. (You wore one of another colour.)
    9. Tina did not say you wore her green <u>jacket</u>. (You wore something else that was green.)

- Watch the student and mimic any useful behaviour to demonstrate that you think it is a sound strategy. For example, if the student is tracking the text with their finger, do the same. Some

teachers will discourage this as being a childish habit in an older student, but whatever helps the student should be considered good practice. Tracking text can maintain student focus and record their place on the page; using a pen or pencil may seem more adult and is also acceptable.
- Ignore minor errors such as the omission or addition of a word, if the mistake does not change the meaning of the passage. It is stressful to know that reading is expected to be perfect. If students know that every minor error will be corrected, they will begin to focus on decoding rather than the higher skill of understanding.

How to prompt

When children first learn to read, they will acquire some phonic knowledge (an understanding of letter-to-sound relationships). When prompting a reader, their phonic knowledge, however limited, can be used to give clues: 'What letters does the word begin/end with?'; 'Can you remember what sound the letters "nch" make at the end of a word?: I'm thinking of: bench, pinch, drench, wrench, lunch and bunch'. 'Ph' at the start of a word can sound like an 'f': Physics, photo, phantom, phone, Phoebe and phew'. Although in 2013, one in seven Year 6 children left primary school without having achieved the expected Level 4 in reading, these children will have had six years of phonics input and are certain to have pockets of understanding.

The following verses illustrate some common problems:

I take it you already know
Of tough and bough and cough and dough?
Others may stumble, but not you,
On hiccough, thorough, lough and through?
Well done! And now you wish, perhaps,
To learn of less familiar traps?
Beware of heard, a dreadful word
That looks like beard and sounds like bird,
And dead: it's said like bed, not bead –
For goodness sake don't call it deed!
Watch out for meat and great and threat
(They rhyme with suite and straight and debt).

A moth is not a moth in mother,
Nor both in bother, broth in brother,
And here is not a match for there
Nor dear and fear for bear and pear,
And then there's dose and rose and lose –
Just look them up – and goose and choose,
And cork and work and card and ward,
And font and front and word and sword,
And do and go and thwart and cart –
Come, come, I've hardly made a start!
A dreadful language? Man alive!
I'd mastered it when I was five!

(Anon)

English is a phonetically irregular language having had input from numerous other languages as it evolved. As secondary students begin to read more complicated texts, an increasing number of phonetically irregular words will be used and there will be need for an additional focus on specialist sight vocabulary. If words the reader does not recognise automatically can be noted down on sets of blank postcards, the cards can be used for revision at the beginning or end of subsequent reading sessions.

- Always give positive feedback. Rather than saying, 'No, you got that wrong', say 'I think that word was on the last page. Let's have a look'.
- If the student gets stuck, prompt them. This can be done in several ways depending on their strengths and the approach being used. If an individual's understanding is good, but the development of decoding is the focus of the lesson, teach them to look at clues within the unknown word: first letters, last letters, smaller words within the word or to make comparisons with similar looking words. If their decoding skills are good, but they need to make more sense of what they are reading, developing comprehension should be the focus, so try:

    o Read the previous sentence(s) aloud with enough exaggerated expression to suggest meaning.
    o Ask a question to direct the student to the correct word.
    o Point out a clue in the illustrations.

- o Suggest the reader tries a word that might fit to see if it would make sense. Does their word match what is happening in the story or accompanying illustrations?
- o Suggest leaving the word out and coming back to it when they have read to the end of the sentence or paragraph.
- o Use grammatical knowledge to narrow down guesses. We know the word is a verb because it refers to what the astronaut is doing. Some students are able to transfer grammatical knowledge they have acquired in French, German, Latin or Spanish lessons to help with English.
- o Give the word immediately, but make a note of it and see if the student can remember it at the end of the session or in the next lesson.

- If the student is making several errors and the reading is in danger of becoming laborious, always give words immediately to maintain fluency.

> The main aim of hearing students read is to hear them read, not to hear them make mistakes.

When the reader comes up against longer, unknown words, demonstrate the use of syllabification. Encourage the student to break words down into syllables or smaller parts: dis/solv/ing, con/den/sa/tion, Medi/terra/nean, Carib/bean, to/get/her. Some students will think the only way to break words down is to sound out each letter separately – c-o-n-d-e-n-s-a-t-i-o-n – and so not even try when told to 'sound the word out'. When looking at syllables, it doesn't matter where the lines between the syllables are drawn: the aim being for the student to realise that words can be broken down into smaller parts. The adult can write the word out in syllables on a piece of paper and then build it up again by saying the parts, slowly at first and then quickly to form the original word. Sometimes the student will recognise the word when it is said, although more unusual words may not be known even when pronounced correctly. Such words need to be recorded and revised during subsequent lessons.

Students may not like to take the time to sound words out when reading aloud in mainstream lessons in case it makes them sound childish. Acknowledge that the technique is perhaps more useful when they are reading to themselves and it doesn't matter how long it takes them to work out a word. However, sounding words out is always a useful fallback strategy.

Developing the student's comprehension

Does the student realise that what they are reading should make sense? Do they monitor their reading, hear when they make an error, go back and re-read in order to self-correct? The student may not realise that they should understand what they read. To some students reading is just one more meaningless exercise initiated by teachers and carried out at school: sometimes you will understand a passage and sometimes you will just say the words.

Many readers experience a plateau in their reading at the end of KS2. They are able to decode the print on the page, but find it more difficult to 'read between the lines' or respond to what they are reading. Their reading skills may remain at this level as they move through secondary education.

Strategies to help support pupil comprehension

- Have an initial discussion about the author, title, cover and blurb of the book in order to 'set the scene' before reading. What does the title suggest about the book? Have you read anything before by this author? What are you expecting the book to be about? What sort of new words might this article contain? Point out to the student that looking at the blurb, author's name and date of publication is always a good strategy: 'If you are going to work for a law firm, checking publication dates will be an essential part of any reading you do. Legal information becomes outdated very quickly.'

- Take time before reading to introduce any unfamiliar vocabulary and discuss relevant background. If the book is about Robin Hood, the reader would need to know about the background of the character and the historical period in which the stories are set. Where is Sherwood Forest, who was the Sheriff of Nottingham and what are the meanings of such words as: venison, longbow, friar, knight, monastery and Norman? Why was Robin Hood an outlaw? Was he a bad person to steal from priests? Without any prior understanding it would be hard for the student to make any sense of the story.
- To check comprehension levels, section the text according to the age and ability of the reader, perhaps reading one or two pages and then discussing what has happened so far. Pausing to summarise information as you read, is a useful technique. Weaker readers may read long sections of text with no understanding and, when asked questions about what they have read, guess rather than make an effort to re-read. Poor decoders who have struggled through a passage reading laboriously word for word will be appalled at the idea of going back over the material to check information. When encouraged to review after a page or two, they will be more likely to retain the required facts.
- Use a timer to read aloud for a certain amount of time, then stop and ask the students for a summary. This approach can be used for silent reading to check comprehension and has additional potential for extending students' reading stamina.
- Discuss word meanings. Create word webs of similar or related words: other words that you might find in an article about space rockets; other words that could be used to describe a cat's fur; words that might be useful to know when reading about the theatre. The development of reading is closely linked to the development of language. If readers do not know what a cat or a mat are, they will not be able to make sense of the sentence, 'The cat sat on the mat'. Many students need language and vocabulary development alongside input to develop reading fluency and accuracy.
- Encourage prediction: What do you think will happen next? What do you think she'll do now? Why do you think that? Chapters with cliff hanger endings will give useful prediction practice. Explain that authors will not spell out all the action and description in a story, but leave a lot to the reader's imagination in order to make their work more interesting.
- Encourage the reader to develop visualisation techniques. Visualisation being the process whereby the reader makes a mental video of the action and the characters in a passage. Some readers read without re-creating the story mentally. Can you see a picture of that scene in your head? What colour armour is the knight wearing in your picture? In your picture, what time of year is it? Is it snowing or stormy? Are the knights in a forest or a field?
- Ask questions to ensure the student understands that text is meant to impart information. Keep questions as open ended as possible to allow the student to think more deeply and to realise that numerous interpretations of the material are possible. What do you think is the author's aim in this chapter? Why do you think the soldiers might be behaving like that? Why do you think the sergeant might have shouted at his men?
- After reading, discuss the plot, characters and events. Why did certain things happen; why did the characters say what they said and what might they do next? This does not have to be an inquisition, but an informal conversation and an opportunity to discuss how we can predict events in fiction using general knowledge, information given in the story, knowledge about the motivations of others and understanding of social issues. Encourage the reader to make sense of the action in the light of their own experience and to relate the story to their own lives. Useful questions to initiate such discussions might include:
    - Have you read other stories where something similar happens?
    - Has anything like that ever happened to you, a friend or a member of your family?
    - Why do you think it happened?
    - Why do you think the driver did that?
    - Is that what you would have done in those circumstances?

(Continued)

(Continued)

- - What do you think will happen next and why?
  - Can you identify the part of the story that makes you think that?
  - What word or group of words support your opinion and why?

- Many fiction texts will have the same story lines with the context, characters and events changed. The more students read, the more they will be able to recognise these patterns. This will help the student to infer what will happen later in the story: will the quiet character come to the fore, save the other characters from a dangerous situation and become a hero? What is the usual outcome in stories like this?
- Ask questions by way of summary to clarify any confusion. What words are new to you in this chapter? Was anything confusing? What do you think the author should have explained more clearly?

Chapter 3

Improving reading through mainstream lessons

This chapter will discuss how to:

- ensure the readability of subject texts matches student's reading age
- support students' reading of non-fiction reading material
- develop students' comprehension
- extend understanding of subject vocabulary
- increase students' reading speed.

Few secondary students would consider working on reading skills to be a worthwhile stand-alone activity. When considering the mass of curriculum information they must cover in preparation for exams, time spent developing generic skills may appear to be time wasted. It can be hard for a student to appreciate that cultivating wider skills will have far-reaching and long-term benefits.

However, when appropriate practice is integrated into mainstream lessons, reading can be developed alongside subject knowledge. When awareness is raised of the many reading opportunities presented in lessons – reading from OHPs, whiteboards or display boards, reading other students' work, reading from the computer screen, reading from worksheets or reading instructions for practical activities – teaching staff could make such opportunities as appropriate as possible for individual pupils.

Ensuring the readability of subject texts matches student's reading age

Teaching staff may be aware that a student has a low reading age, yet have a limited understanding of the implications of this for the classroom. If a Year 11 student has a reading age of a Year 6 student, their academic performance is certain to be affected, although not always in an obvious way. The *Sun* newspaper is said to have a readability level of 9 years (that is, the paper could be read by someone with a 9-year-old child's reading ability), and the *Guardian* newspaper a level of 16 years. However, if a student wanted to read an article of personal interest, possessed adequate background knowledge and was familiar with the specialist vocabulary used, they would be able to read material beyond their supposed competence. When reading material holds no personal interest, students prefer to read below their competence level. When a student is required to read such material independently and with comprehension, the reading level of the text would need to be two years below their theoretical reading level.

> Measuring a student's reading age will only provide approximate guidance about the appropriateness of reading material. There are other factors that affect the ease with which a text can be read: prior knowledge of the topic, student motivation and understanding of specialist vocabulary.

The readability of subject texts

Betts (1946) discussed the concept of independent, instructional and frustration reading levels. An independent level of reading would require the reader to have an understanding of the material content and be able to read the text with 95 per cent accuracy. An instructional level of reading would mean the student would be able to read with 90–94 per cent accuracy and understand the content of the text with minimal support, perhaps through the pre-teaching of a few unfamiliar words. A frustration level of reading would mean the reader would make one decoding error in every ten words and have little understanding of text content. At the frustration level of reading, decoding would engage all the reader's attention with little energy left to focus on comprehension. If the book is one the students wish or need to read, but is in advance of the reading capability of some of the class, the text could be read chorally. This would enable weaker readers to divert their energy from decoding towards comprehension.

The readability levels of secondary school textbooks will vary; some classic English texts will have a readability level in advance of all of the students' chronological age. In addition to a high reading age, such texts may be written in unfamiliar forms of English. For example, this extract from Jane Austen's *Pride and Prejudice* (Chapter 24):

> You shall not, for the sake of one individual, change the meaning of principle and integrity, nor endeavour to persuade yourself or me, that selfishness is prudence, and insensibility of danger security for happiness.
>
> (*Pride and Prejudice*, Ch. 24)

The problem of unfamiliar language will be apply to texts from all subjects, such as the following from a GCSE Maths course text:

> For both indefinite and definite integrals, any more complex integrand must be simplified before you attempt to integrate. You need to write it in the same form as you do for differentiation, that is, a string of terms in the form $ax^b \pm cx^d$.

It would be disheartening for a student to be expected to read and understand such material without their reading ability being taken into account and soul destroying if the student could complete the task set if they were able to decode the instructions. Such students would be unable to access the wider learning experience on a regular basis simply as a direct result of inadequate reading skills.

There are numerous tests that measure the readability level of material. These include the SMOG test (see below), in addition to online programs such as MS Word 2007 and 2010, which have readability statistics available under 'proofing' in Word Options. The tests involve calculations based on the number of complex sentences and polysyllabic words in a passage.

SMOG assessment

- Select a sample of 30 sentences from the text.
- Count the number of words with more than three syllables in the sample.
- Divide the number of polysyllabic words by the number of sentences to give 'N'
- The reading age of the passage = the square root of 'N' + 8 years.

Some material, for example, a Physics textbook, will have a high readability level because of the number of polysyllabic subject words the text contains.

One simple way to test the suitability of a book for students is the 'Five finger test'. Place a finger on each word readers are unable to decode on a page and if there are more than five such words, i.e., you run out of fingers, the text is too difficult for the students. For books with more text, use a 5 per cent decoding rule. To assess a text for a specific group use a cloze passage: photocopy a section of 100 words from half way through the book and blank out every seventh word. If the readers can make sense of the version with the blanks, they will be able to understand the text.

Readability levels apply to worksheets as well as textbooks. Worksheets will present an additional challenge when they are poorly copied, have complex sentence structure, a mass of condensed text, unfamiliar words or introduce too many new concepts on the same sheet. When worksheets are well designed, students are provided with an additional opportunity to practise reading in a meaningful way.

> **Strategies to aid readability of worksheets**
>
> - If the layout of the worksheet is complicated, it will seem overwhelming to a weak reader. The text may appear too hard for them to decode, too long for them to finish in the time allowed, too complex for them to understand. If the text is uncluttered with clear headings and information chunked into sections, it will instantly be seen as more accessible.
> - Plain English should be used and jargon avoided.
> - Sentences should be short and straightforward.
> - Bullet points and numbering are useful to link different sections of material.
> - Left-aligned text is preferable. Words split between different lines make it difficult for the reader to carry decoding into the next sentence.
> - The use of lower case letters is preferable. Use capitals at the beginning of sentences, but not for whole words. For many readers the shape of words gives valuable decoding clues: capillary written in lower case being a more distinctive shape than CAPILLARY.
> - Use a simple font, ideally sans serif, to ensure the print is as clear as possible and without any distracting loops or tails to letters. There is an argument that a visually complex font will make the reader focus more, but this will not apply to the easily de-motivated reader.
> - Use font of an adequate size, 12–18 point is preferable, in order to avoid eyestrain.
> - Do not print over any diagrams or pictures as this will make the layout visually confusing.
> - Pale blue or green paper may be preferable to white paper for some students. Do not use paper that is either too dark or glossy as this can add a visual problem to a reading problem.
> - Subject keyword displays are useful, particularly when images are supplied to enable students to access definitions quickly. Lists of keywords are best displayed at the bottom of the sheet, so the student does not have to flick from page to page in order to look up words. A subject keyword dictionary may seem a time-consuming way to look up words, but can be useful in some situations.
> - Pictures, graphs, charts and annotated diagrams giving a visual representation of written information help to support reading. The expression, 'A picture paints a thousand words', is true for many.

It is never a question of watering down the original information. Teachers must ensure students can access texts in a meaningful way, understanding the original, whilst acquiring the techniques necessary to use with similar texts in the future.

> The readability of a text can be instantly improved when unfamiliar specialist language is explained, main points identified and connections made with previous learning.

Supporting students' reading of non-fiction reading material

In secondary school the language and structure of written texts will steadily increase in complexity. If a student's vocabulary and experience of the structure of advanced material is limited and their general knowledge poor, there will be subject texts they are able to decode, but not understand. As students move through secondary school, they will come in contact with an increasing diversity of such texts. The majority of early reading material is fiction, so subject texts may seem less familiar and bring different challenges: specialist vocabulary, density of material, length and complexity of sentences and the inclusion of annotations, facts boxes, diagrams and illustrations.

When tackling non-fiction text, the reader will need to be aware of:

- The different parts of the book: chapters, index, glossary and blurb.
- Different text features: titles, captions, insets and sidebars.
- The index and how it is used to peruse specific topics of interest.
- The date of publication. The information may be out of date and therefore irrelevant.
- The structure of the chapter. Is there a summary that could be used before reading to check whether the chapter will be of interest?
- The glossary. Is it accessible and easily understood?
- Visual displays, diagrams, charts, illustrations and charts. Are they helpful or confusing? If they look confusing, the book probably will not meet the reader's needs.
- The layout of the book. If the print is too small, the text dense and the vocabulary challenging, the text will not be appropriate for the reader's needs.

Appropriate reading techniques for non-fiction material

It is essential to teach weaker readers to review before they start reading: Why am I reading this? Is the whole text relevant or should I just read sections? What do I need to know and what type of reading should I be doing? Reviewing will help the students to read effectively, reducing the likelihood of feeling overwhelmed by the quantity of the material. Such skills can be taught by modelling, that is, by the adult talking the students through strategies used by competent readers.

It is generally accepted that competent readers use three techniques to access information from non-fiction texts: skimming, scanning and close reading.

Skimming involves looking quickly through a book or part of a book to see if it contains the information required or other information that might be useful. Skimming a text immediately reduces the quantity to be read with any irrelevant material rejected. The reader focuses on: titles, chapter headings, introductions, summaries, emboldened information, diagrams or illustrations.

It is worth pointing out to students that:

- Paragraphs will mark the introduction of a new idea.
- The first sentence is usually the topic sentence and will tell the reader what the paragraph is about.
- The reader should focus their attention on information words rather than decode every word.

Scanning is when the reader looks for specific information within a text: a particular historical event or character, the date of a concert or specific information about transpiration, volcanoes or greenhouse gases. The reader needs to be able to use the index, chapter headings, summaries, glossaries and tables in order to focus their search.

It is worth pointing out to students that:

- Dates will be numbers and so will stand out from the text.
- Names of places and people will be proper nouns and easier to find because they will start with capital letters.

- If they are scanning a text in order to answer questions set by the teacher, it can be assumed that the first question will refer to the first section of text, information relating to the next question be slightly further into the passage and so on.

Close reading involves careful reading, word for word, in order to understand the material. This can be difficult for students if they have little interest in the topic. It is easy for them to drift away, lose concentration and find they have 'read' several pages, but cannot remember a single word. As they get older, the need to read for subjects in which they have little or no interest will be reduced, but most secondary students will be taking a range of subjects and a lack of intrinsic interest in some is inevitable.

It is worth pointing out to students that:

- If they are to maintain concentration, they will need to learn to **read actively**.

Active reading

Active reading involves engagement with the text; reading passages aloud, highlighting specific parts of the text, listening to someone else reading the text, asking themselves questions – Was the information clearly presented? What did I learn? – and discussing the information with others and/or making summary notes.

- **Note making.** Encourage students to make notes *after* they have read a passage. If they put their pens down as they read, they will not be tempted to copy directly from the text, but give themselves time to think about the content and then record their thoughts in their own words. Notes made in this way will make more sense when referred to at a later date. Regular reviewing and recording after every few pages is a sensible approach: breaks will give the reader time to review the information and make sense of it in the light of what they already know. Reading on regardless of levels of understanding is likely to leave the reader feeling overwhelmed and confused. If students are encouraged to identify the main idea in a passage and then look for supporting detail, they can record the overview in an alternative format, perhaps a mind map, comic strip or a time line.
- **SQ3R.** One interactive approach to reading is known as the SQ3R (Survey, Question, Read, Recall, Review) method. The student is taught the following routine: *Survey* the text to get an overview, looking through the index and text for key words. *Question* as to whether the whole book or only certain chapters need to be read. *Read* at a rate that ensures comprehension. *Recall* information to check understanding. *Review* to ensure that all relevant information has been collected.
- **PQRS** is a similar process (Preview, Question, Read and Summarise). Teaching students to use these types of scaffolding for reading activities will help weaker readers to do what good readers do automatically.

Developing comprehension

Comprehension will mean different things to different people. In its broadest sense, comprehension is a life skill and in its narrowest sense, an isolated exercise carried out in English lessons. Classroom comprehension exercises test a student's current level of ability, but do not always help the student to develop their skills. Many readers experience a plateau at the end of Year 4 or 5 when they are able to decode the print on

> Decoding is the basis of learning to read, but the primary purpose of reading is comprehension.

the page, but find it difficult to 'read between the lines' or to respond to what they read. They may be at this level when they transfer to secondary education. If these students are to improve their comprehension, they need to be taught to engage actively with reading.

Fiction

In order to comprehend fiction, the reader requires:

- **An adequate vocabulary.** The complexity of the vocabulary used in reading material will increase as students move through secondary school and meaning will be lost if readers are confronted with too many unfamiliar words. The situation would be akin to a reader discovering that half of the words in a text are in another language. An adequate vocabulary is important for all school subjects. This will include both Arts and Science subjects, as tasks set in Maths and Science lessons are often couched in language in order to give questions relevance to everyday life.
- **An understanding of the conventions of print.** It is possible to read gibberish if the reader understands how texts are structured, as the following example demonstrates:

    It is kwite possibel to raed this txet with a graet many mistakes becos we no hwat we expetc to raed: teh sense is ont afectid untl we distreb teh construction of teh language.

- **An understanding of the interaction of grammar and text.** The reader needs to appreciate the grammatical conventions of text, to know that a full stop marks the end of a sentence, a question mark indicates when a question is being asked and speech marks show when someone is talking. The grammatical structure of a sentence will help the reader anticipate the type of word that follows: 'The child ran out into the ___'; 'The dog began to gnaw at the ___'. The student who understands basic grammar will know the missing words must be nouns rather than verbs, adjectives or prepositions.
- **An adequate general knowledge.** The vital role played by general knowledge in comprehension is often over looked. The student has to be able to make sense of text content within their knowledge of the world. If they are to understand the story of the Three Little Pigs at the simplest level, readers need to know that a wolf would want to eat a pig, a brick house would be stronger than a straw or stick house, boiling water scalds and that a chimney will lead from a roof down to a fireplace. If a student's experience of the world is restricted, they will have problems with basic comprehension. EAL readers will often experience similar problems because they lack cultural general knowledge and are unaware of social norms.
- **An understanding of the different genres of texts.** What does the reader already know about this specific genre? Is it a short story, poem or a letter and how should it be read? What format do these sorts of texts usually take? The student will need to be shown how to read material and make predictions about what will happen next based on their current understanding, accepting their predictions may change when the author reveals new information. Authors often make their work more interesting by asking their readers to make inferences from the information given and to predict what will happen next. Encourage students to identify this technique and to read on to see if their assumptions are proved correct. To make inferences the reader is required to deduce meaning from clues given in the material and then make links with their own life experiences. It is possible to draw on an understanding of the structure of different texts to focus predictions, such as: 'In other stories by this author, the villain is revealed in the final chapter to be the character that seemed to be the hero's friend'; 'Animals in stories often rescue characters who have been cruel to them'; or 'The victim usually helps the bully in this type of story'.

Non-fiction

Non-fiction texts require an understanding of different constructions of text: subject vocabulary, layout and design with the inclusion of grids, charts, graphs, quotes, examples, bullet points, illustrations, lists, annotations, titles and small boxes of text. The teacher may need to model how to glean information from such features and enable the student to identify the main points in a text, recognising that other information has been added for interest, but does not affect the main argument.

With non-fiction, there is an expectation that the text is there to be understood. Good readers will clarify their purpose in reading, identify the important aspects of the text, concentrate on understanding the overview rather than trivia, monitor reading to check their understanding, take action when they are uncertain of information and maximise concentration on the task in hand. Those students who work through text as if they were reading a shopping list may not realise that the words should convey meaning. They may be used to reading words they do not know and are unconcerned when they do not understand. Good readers are constantly monitoring their comprehension, deciding whether it is necessary to read all the text carefully or whether to skim for general meaning. As they read, they judge whether or not they have understood a passage and if this matters; should they re-read, look up a few unfamiliar words or would it be better to read on, perhaps looking for a visual display of the confusing information? They understand instinctively that they need to engage actively with texts.

Such strategies may not be obvious to weaker readers, who could assume that it is quite normal not to understand what you have read. If they have decoded it (read the words), then surely they have 'read' it? For some students reading is a difficult, rather pointless activity done in complete isolation and of little relevance to anything else in their life. Others will know they should understand, but feel too embarrassed to ask for help. In both scenarios the teacher may be unaware of the problem.

Students need to question themselves as they read. Weak readers may wait to be asked questions after they have finished reading and then look back in the text for answers. The teacher should model self-questioning whilst reading. Do I agree with what the author is saying in this article? What does the author want me to think about this? It is important that students can develop the ability to recognise bias and be able to separate fact from opinion in order to maintain their independence of thought and be discerning about the opinions of others. How can I tell what is important in this material? Have I lost the drift of the argument? Am I following the sequence of events properly? The student could be asked to note down one question or a reaction every time they finish a page to get used to thinking as they read, such as: 'I don't agree with what the author is saying here'; 'That makes sense because of what was said earlier'; or 'That seems a bit confusing: I'll read to the end of the chapter and see if it becomes clearer.'

A reasonable memory is also a key component to comprehension. It does not stand alone, but relies on the reader's ability to concentrate, reason and order information. When an individual reads, they have to remember what they have read previously if they are to make sense of the sequence of events. Poor readers will focus on decoding and have little capacity left to follow overall meaning. Active reading will help with memory and comprehension.

Different ways to support reading comprehension

Teacher modelling using scaffolds

When readers' comprehension is weak, it will be helpful for the teacher to talk through their own thought processes and model reading approaches to use in different situations. This can be made clear to the student by the adult 'thinking' aloud: 'I am sure Charlotte will go back to her mother's house and ignore what the factory owner is saying.' Then at the end of the next paragraph, 'Oh maybe she won't, I had forgotten that the factory owner knows about Charlotte's brother stealing the bread. Maybe he'll try to blackmail her? Let's see what happens at the end of the chapter.'

The adult can model what they would do when unsure whether or not they had understood the text correctly. How they would use guesswork based on context or knowledge of similar texts, re-read the difficult sections, look up unfamiliar words or imagine they are the characters in the text and think how they might react in a similar situation. For example, 'I don't think I quite understood that bit' (re-read section of text slowly). 'Oh, I see what she means now. She's saying that ...' (summarise meaning in own words).

This process is sometimes referred to as 'RAP': *Read* the passage. *Ask* yourself what it means. *Put* the information into your own words.

> **Modelling example**
>
> The teacher models a suitable approach to take when tackling unseen text by using a photocopied passage from a subject book or newspaper article. Simple or complex text can be used as is appropriate to the individual or group. As the teacher talks through what she is doing and why, the students follow using their own photocopy.
>
> - I (the teacher) read the title or heading to get an idea of the topic and how it fits into what I already know.
> - Then I read the first two sentences to get an idea of what the passage will be about, highlighting any keywords that relate to this topic.
> - I then read the rest of the passage to find the supporting evidence, which I highlight in another colour.
> - After reading, I summarise the main ideas to myself. It might be necessary to examine a text closely to work out the correct sequence of information. (Newspaper obituaries provide good practice for sequencing the order of events in famous people's lives.)
> - Finally, I jot down the gist of the information in my own words.
>
> The students prepare a second summary using the same method with an alternative piece of text. This can be completed individually, in pairs or a small group.

Additional summarising activities include the following:

- Demonstrate how to look for summaries at the beginning and end of chapters in subject textbooks.
- Photocopy newspaper articles for students to summarise in twenty words.
- Give students a report of a sports match to summarise in less than six words as a newspaper headline.
- Ask students to retell stories in their own words, the main events and their responses. This will encourage them to separate the sequence of action in the story from issues raised by the text.
- To practise separating fact from opinion, ask students to examine film or television reviews from newspapers or magazines. Highlight facts and personal opinions in different colours to encourage the students to recognise the difference.

Reading comprehension requires practice using a variety of texts: magazines, printed material from everyday life (application forms, catalogues, and schedules), reference books, newspapers, poems and prose, play scripts, as well as subject textbooks, and a range of fiction material. When comprehension techniques are modelled with subject material in mainstream lessons, activities will appear more purposeful and students are more likely to apply the strategies in the future.

EXIT scaffolding example

Scaffolding was one of the strategies introduced into the classroom in the EXEL Project, (Exeter Extending Literacy project), developed at the University of Exeter School of Education in the 1990s. The EXIT (Extending Interactions with Text) model grew out of the EXEL Project.

The teacher chooses an interesting piece of text, ideally a double-page spread that includes some information displayed visually: a graph, cartoon, time line or pie chart.

1. **Activating the students' prior knowledge** of the topic, perhaps other material read, personal experiences, a film or a television programme. Encourage discussion: 'This reminds me of ...'; 'I once read about ...'; 'That happened to my auntie ...'; 'When my Dad was a boy ...'. This will enable the student to assimilate the personal experiences and prior knowledge of others. Confident readers will instinctively set the scene for themselves, previewing material and asking themselves questions about the subject matter. What do I know already about this topic? What do I need to find out? Have I ever experienced something similar? Am I going to understand this easily because I'm interested in fishing/Roman History/*Star Wars*/hockey? Does this book remind me of anything I've read previously? Less confident readers will start reading without this sort of preparation.
2. **Establishing a purpose** for the activity by question-setting, KWL or QUADS grids. A KWL grid is one example of a graphic organiser (a record of information in diagrammatic form). The KWL grid will have one column for what is *known* about a topic, a second for what the reader *wants* to know and a third to record what has been *learnt* after reading. A QUADS grid has four headings for the students to record information under: Question, Answer, Detail and Source. Such approaches will help the reader focus on their reason for reading and record their results appropriately.
3. **Locating the information** in the texts by skim reading headings, charts, maps and pictures to get an idea of what aspects of a topic the material will cover.
4. **Adopting appropriate strategies** for working with the text through teacher modelling. 'This section needs close reading, but these boxes can be scanned'; 'I'll skim this section; I don't think it's very important'.
5. **Interacting with the text** through text marking and restructuring:

   - Highlight any dates, names and numbers.
   - Underline any unfamiliar words.
   - Use suffixes, prefixes, word families and context to work out the meanings of unfamiliar words.
   - Summarise the main idea. What is the material really about: reasons for the outbreak of the First World War, the functions of the liver, Shakespeare's plays or how volcanoes were formed?
   - Identify any supporting details, looking for any further information to clarify the main point(s).

6. **Monitoring understanding** through teacher modelling, for example, self-questioning.
7. **Recording information**. What would be the best way to summarise this information? The teacher could demonstrate how to pick out the main facts, perhaps using a graphic organiser such as a mind map, chapter summary or concept map to help the reader to get an overview. Have I recorded all necessary information? Is it clear and easy to understand?
8. **Evaluating information**. What have I learnt from this? Does it make sense and link with what I already know?
9. **Assisting memory** by reviewing, revisiting and restructuring. How could I present the information to make it memorable?
10. **Communicating the information** to others by writing in a range of genres, writing frames, poetry, drama, and other alternative outcomes. Ask the students to record the main idea and any supporting information in an alternative format: a time line, mind map, pie chart, comic strip or a linear list.

Another scaffolding method that can be used to read a non-fiction book in a purposeful way is the **SQ3R** (Survey, Question, Read, Recall, Review), enabling the student to make sense of and structure the information. The teacher models the technique and the students practise the process individually or in small groups:

- *Survey.* Look at the title and glance through the contents page and chapter headings to make sure that the book contains the information needed and establish context.
- *Question.* Why am I reading this? What do I need to find out? Which part is going to be most useful?
- *Read.* Read a targeted chapter thinking about key words, and looking closely at any illustrations, graphs or diagrams.
- *Recall.* Think about the chapter and what has been learnt, note down key facts, relate the information to prior knowledge and examples from everyday life.
- *Review.* Check that appropriate information has been taken from the book, recorded and understood.

Change written text into a diagram

This could be with information taken from a class text, magazine or newspaper. The process of thinking about written information and how to convert it into a visual format will ensure students interact with the facts. Examples could include: plotting the career of a famous sporting or historical figure onto a time line; converting written information about the development of a geographical feature into diagrams; displaying the sequence of historical events in a comic strip or illustrating the relationship between characters in a play or set book in a mind map.

Use drama to develop understanding of texts

Acting out texts will assist student comprehension; teach the pronunciation of unfamiliar vocabulary and make material more memorable. If students perform as a character, their understanding of the individual's personality and motivation will be enhanced. The acting does not have to be production level, but performed in small groups to allow everyone to be involved.

Allow students to read in pairs or small groups if necessary to make the experience less daunting. It would be cruel to ask an unwilling reader to read aloud in front of all their peers.

Put the text on the whiteboard for choral reading. Use colour to highlight different parts with different fonts and background colours to add emphasis, emotion and tone. Split the class into groups with each group reading different parts or sections of the material.

Incorporate physical actions and exaggerated speech into the reading. The reader needs to be aware of the conventions of texts: the use of italics, repetition, brackets, exclamation marks and words in bold font and how they give clues about how the passage is to be read and where emphasis is to be placed. If students can act out a text, they will be helped to see how the author intended the work to be read. Words within brackets could become whispered asides, questions stressed by raised, outstretched hands, and emboldened words accompanied by a stamp.

Visualising the passage

Visualisation is one of the approaches good readers use instinctively, changing written content into mental images. To teach the visualisation process:

- The students read a passage of text or it is read to them. The teacher then draws some simple pictures on the whiteboard to show the action in the passage and explain how the pictures relate to the text. The teacher asks questions about the passage and the students use the pictures to help them to recall the desired information.

- The activity is repeated: a different passage is read, the students draw a few simple pictures to represent the sequence of the text. The pictures are discussed and then removed and the students answer questions about the passage using their memory of the pictures to help their recall.
- The students practise the techniques using mental, rather than the drawn, images.

DARTs (Directed Activity Related to Texts)

Directed Activities Related to Text were originally devised by Gardner and Kunzer in the 1970s and 1980s to try to increase students' interaction with non-fiction texts and improve their comprehension. The approach was deemed necessary because students are able to answer superficial reading comprehension questions with no deep understanding. The following is an example:

They watched as the Slopger frumpt across the buzzling vernan.

Question: How did the Slopger cross the vernan?

Answer: The Slopger frumpt across the vernan.

Question: What was the vernan like?

Answer: The vernan was buzzling.

DARTs are designed to make the reader think more deeply about the text. The activities give the teacher important feedback as if students are unable to complete tasks, they have not understood the passage read. The activities are popular with students because they see them as interesting games and puzzles, they are able to take the initiative in working through the tasks and, as there are several possible answers for each activity, they feel able to tackle more challenging reading material.

When DARTs are used in subject lessons, they are seen by students as relevant tasks. Comprehension exercises that are unrelated to subjects can appear removed from curriculum content: readers' background knowledge of topics will be variable, so their understanding will be compromised. If, for example, a comprehension task is about American Football, the reader without an understanding of the game will be at an immediate disadvantage. However, if a DARTs activity refers to the Water Table, everyone who had been in the lesson relating to the Water Table should be able to complete the activity.

DARTs can be divided into two broad categories, reconstruction and analysis. *Reconstruction* activities involve the students working with texts that have been broken down and have to be reassembled. *Analysis* activities involve the selection of information from unmodified texts. Typical DART activities would include: cloze work, table or diagram completion, text restructuring, table or diagram construction, summarising and text marking:

- Cloze exercises might consist of sections of text with keywords or phrases removed for the student to replace: the student has to understand context and vocabulary in order to identify the correct words or type of words. As students move through secondary school, texts will increase in complexity with answers to comprehension questions dependent on the students' appreciation of complex sentence structure and knowledge of grammar. Without an understanding of grammar and punctuation, a student will not be able to read with expression or make sense of a passage. A cloze exercise will give the teacher an opportunity to demonstrate the specific structures that different texts take.
- Sequencing tasks will require the reader to read texts several times, paying attention to structure, vocabulary and the correct order of information.
- Restructuring will necessitate reading the text critically, working out what information is relevant and what is not, then summarising and presenting the information in alternative ways.
- Text marking will require the reader to use different techniques, to find the main ideas of the piece and sort them into order of relevance, perhaps highlighting the main ideas in one colour and supporting details in other colours.

Extending understanding of subject vocabulary

> As subject vocabulary becomes more complex, it is vital that students keep pace. If they are not developing their vocabulary at a similar rate, it will be easy for their reading comprehension levels to drop as they progress through school.

Unfamiliar words in fiction may not impede student understanding to the same extent as unfamiliar words in non-fiction material. However, specialist vocabulary can be made more accessible through support in mainstream lessons. Teaching staff may suspect poor understanding of subject vocabulary when they observe students: using words without understanding; not recalling words; only remembering part of a word; remembering words in one context, but not being able to generalise their use; finding words relating to abstract contexts particularly difficult or by being easily confused with words of similar meanings. Students need to access the correct vocabulary and hear it used in context before they will understand it in text. It will not help to use simpler language as paraphrasing does not always make the message easier to understand, for example, 'electricity' being a more useful and concise term than the phrase 'the power that comes out of a plug'. Advanced vocabulary condenses concepts and helps students to structure their thoughts succinctly.

Strategies to increase student familiarity with subject vocabulary

1. Before reading a text, highlight any complex words for the students to try to pronounce and define. This will provide a useful overview of text content as well as revision opportunities for subject vocabulary. Words and their definitions could be recorded separately at the back of the student's files.
2. Create keyword booklets. These could be designed within departments for every year group or for different topics and modules. Year group dictionaries could be produced with departments identifying keywords for their particular section or the vocabulary that students will need to know for different topics. Lists should not be over long and definitions clear and student friendly. They could be produced as A4 sheets for students' folders, as inserts for planners or printed as bookmarks. Learning from vocabulary lists could be a homework task with the students' knowledge of the words checked during introductory or plenary sessions.
3. Classroom displays. The keyword booklets as described above could form the basis for classroom wall displays and referred to during lessons.
4. Several publishers, for example, Peppermint Publications (www.peppermintpublications.co.uk) produce subject vocabulary resources that include vocabulary games, crosswords, word searches and matching activities. These are accessible activities that provide valuable homework activities and will give feedback on student understanding.
5. If classroom vocabulary displays are large enough, they can be used for choral activities, with the whole class chanting the words and their definitions. This can give valuable, yet discreet, practice for those students who are uncertain of the pronunciation of the words. Syllables within the words can be exaggerated to aid memory.
6. Display topic vocabulary word maps on classroom notice boards and use them for classroom discussion, for example:

   - Volcano words – lava, gases, ash, crater, conical, igneous, magma, vent or activity.
   - Coastal erosion words – wave, currents, sediment, abrasion, dunes, tidal, beach, columns or pillar.
   - Electricity words – static, charge, volts, field, amperes, waves, electromagnetic or current.

7. Use subject-specific vocabulary during lessons, but do not assume that all students will remember the words or their meanings immediately. Students need to see and hear a word pronounced several times before it becomes part of their vocabulary and recognised automatically in texts. In the same way that names of football teams, places or first names (Leicester City, Meopham, Vaughan, Siobhan, Daphne), can prove difficult to decode at first, they will become a flow of familiar sounds after regular use. Seeing a phonetic version of a word or a visual clue as to its correct pronunciation may be necessary until the readers' recall is automatic.
8. When reading fiction, names of characters that sound similar may be easily confused. Supply students with a list of characters and the part they play in the text to keep at the back of their file. The students may not have pronounced the names when reading silently, but recognise the name by its shape: long name with 'gh' in the middle, very short name beginning with 'Jal', name that looks like 'Lizzy'. The first time they have to pronounce the word when reading aloud may cause embarrassment and they may need to be shown tricks of how to remember unusual pronunciations until their recall is secure.
9. Revise basic topic vocabulary by using earlier Key Stage books to revisit common subject keywords and consolidate understanding. Occasionally at the beginning of lessons, take time to review any subject words and definitions students have experienced difficulty with in the past.
10. Use IT for online definitions and interactive glossaries.
11. Give homework that provides extra opportunities to revise subject vocabulary: cloze procedures, word searches, crosswords, puzzles. Word games can be used as part of preparation for new modules: quick quizzes, bingo, Pictionary, odd man out, loop cards, oral dominoes or DARTs activities. A lesson plenary may give a few minutes to introduce this sort of activity.
12. Revise instruction words that are used in exam questions. All pupils sitting public examinations need to be familiar with this vocabulary:

- *Analyse*: Take apart a concept or a process, and explain it step by step.
- *Compare*: Show likenesses and differences when comparing two events, theories, or processes.
- *Contrast*: Show differences between two processes or theories.
- *Define*: Provide a definition of a key term.
- *Demonstrate*: Provide proof of your answer by using an example.
- *Discuss*: Demonstrate that you know the strengths and weaknesses of both sides of an argument.
- *Explain*: Provide an answer that gives a 'why' response. Give an overview of the problem and a solution for a particular issue.
- *Illustrate*: Use examples to show or explain a topic.
- *Justify*: Use examples or evidence to show why (in your opinion) information is correct.
- *Order*: Provide a chronological or value-based answer by listing several items, terms or events in correct placement.
- *Relate*: Show a relationship between two events or items by discussing their similarities.
- *Prove*: Use evidence (this could be numbers) or reasoning to solve a problem.

To maximise pupils' achievement in exams, it will be essential to practise answering questions from old papers. Students may have revised thoroughly and have perfect recall of all required information, but if they do not understand what response a question requires, they will underperform. This is often the case for pupils who do well in coursework and lessons, but regularly underachieve in school tests and examinations. They won't know why their test results are poor and will blame inadequate revision or lack of effort, trying to cram more, not realising that their problems lie elsewhere.

Increasing student reading speed

Students' reading speeds will vary considerably across the same year group. One of the easiest ways to demonstrate this is to ask the class to read silently from a class textbook or reader for a minute, reading carefully enough to be able to answer questions afterwards. The students then count the number of words they have read to get an approximate 'words per minute' score. It is important that this is done individually or the students may compare scores and change their results to put them in line with their peers. If the task is carried out anonymously and for interest only, the students can be asked to jot down their result on a piece of paper. There will be such a wide range of scores within every teaching group that staff will be forced to think carefully about setting independent reading for homework. It will be apparent that some students will take three or four times longer than their peers to complete a reading task. The temptation for slower readers to ignore reading homework, particularly if it is of no obvious relevance, may be too great to be ignored.

> Reading is about understanding and not about speed.

Before starting to teach speed reading techniques, it is necessary to investigate why a student is reading slowly.

We read to understand information, not to read quickly. Increasing a student's reading speed would be pointless if improvements in speed resulted in a decline in comprehension.

Reading requires a level of active awareness and thought about language which diminishes when reading speed is emphasized. A literate person is one who derives meaning, not speed, from the printed word.

(Rasinski and Hamman, 2010)

The average speed for an adult to read a straight forward text is between 300 and 400 words per minute. When reading more challenging texts, their speed may drop to between 230 and 250 words per minute. Different types of texts require different approaches. Students need to be taught to skim material and ask themselves if it is necessary to read all of the text or to scan for specific pieces of information looking at introductory passages and summaries. If the student is taught to use such strategies, they will be able to reduce immediately the quantity of material to be read.

At the end of Year 1 some students will be reading at a rate of 15 words per minute and others at 100+ words per minute. By Year 6 students' reading speed will vary from 93 words per minute to 204 words per minute (Hasbrouck and Tindal, 2006).

An average secondary school student will read an accessible text at approximately 200–250 words per minute. If secondary students are reading easy texts silently at a speed of below 100 words a minute, it will be worth analysing why this might be. When faced with reading a classical novel for KS3 English, a student who reads silently at the same pace with which they read aloud is certain to become discouraged and bored.

Why students are slow readers

- Students may have ongoing problems with the automatic recognition of keywords. They will need regular practice of keyword recall.
- Students may have limited vocabulary and general knowledge. Reading speed will be reduced when the reader has to stop to consider the meanings of words or sections of texts. A large number of unfamiliar words or poor general knowledge will affect comprehension as the reader struggles to make sense of a passage whilst retaining overall meaning. Increasing an individual's vocabulary and improving general knowledge will be more of a priority in such cases.
- If the readers have weak memories, the previous two points will put an extra burden on their memory at a time when the comprehension of the reading material should be paramount.

- Some readers will read at the same speed from habit and may get into a reading speed rut they are unable to break out of. All children will read aloud initially when they first start to decode. As they become more confident, they will begin to read silently, but will continue to say the words in their heads. Later when they become fluent readers, they will convert words to meaning without changing them into speech. Some slow readers may not have achieved this final level of competence and still need to be given regular opportunities to read aloud to increase their automatic fluency. Reading is an activity that is certain to improve with regular practice and many students continue to need reading practice throughout secondary school.
- Other readers believe they can only understand a text when they hear it. They continue to read aloud because they feel it is the only way for them to absorb information. They will need to be taught to use different reading approaches for different activities.
- Some individuals will have poor concentration and feel they have to read slowly and keep re-reading because they lose focus. They worry that their comprehension will be compromised if they don't read carefully. However, reading quickly can help maintain focus: the reader knows they have to concentrate for a short period and cannot afford to let their attention drift.
- The students may not read complex texts very often and have problems with the length and complexity of sentence structure. Advanced texts will include prepositional phrases and adverbial clauses that may confuse the less confident reader. The more frequently the student tackles this sort of text, the sooner they will become familiar with the layout. Initially it will help if they are encouraged to read advanced texts relating to a subject of personal interest until their level of competence develops.
- Students may use the same techniques for all types of reading activity. They have just one reading speed (slow), and don't realise that there are several ways of reading and that a magazine article is read in a different way to a Physics textbook. Good readers automatically vary their reading speed according to the difficulty of the text, their reason for reading and familiarity with the material. Slow, word by word reading is an essential part of some tasks, perhaps when reading from a condensed, complicated Economics textbook, but would be a nonsensical approach to use when flicking through a magazine. Once students enter secondary school it is essential that they are able to read quickly to get the general idea of the text rather than to decode every word. If they are to increase their reading speed, they must be taught a range of approaches to take when reading different types of texts.

Strategies to increase reading speed

- Suggest the student uses a pencil to track steadily down the page, moving the eyes down and across the text at the speed of the pencil. Reading at this sort of constant pace will improve comprehension as the reader knows they have to focus on the sentence they are reading and their eyes mustn't be distracted by words above or below. Gradually increase the speed of pencil movement.
- The same sort of exercise as above can be carried out using a ruler to move steadily from line to line down the page. (This may not be as useful because the length of the ruler will encourage the reader to look at more words.)
- Use a finger to move down the centre of the page in a zigzag movement, not focusing on the beginnings or endings of lines, unless a complex word catches the eye. Keep the finger moving smoothly down the page and do not allow the eyes to regress. The brain will learn to fill any gaps in the information received.
- Do not allow any silent speech or sub-vocalising. This is where the individual is reading word for word quietly as if reading aloud. This habit will slow the reading process down as it takes longer to pronounce the words rather than recognise them. To break this habit, try chewing gum whilst reading or holding a biro between the teeth.

(Continued)

(Continued)

- Slow readers read one word at a time; faster readers take in groups of four or five words at a time. Encourage readers to practise looking at groups of words rather than individual ones.
- Experiment with the use of different coloured overlays to reduce visual discomfort. Change the background colour of the computer screen or photocopy texts on pastel coloured paper. Some readers find black print on white paper visually uncomfortable, complaining of glare or moving print. The use of coloured or off-white paper for worksheets and coloured overlays for texts seems to reduce the problem for some. Coloured overlays can be made from the plastic transparent A4 dividers that can be purchased from most stationery shops.
- If students are reading from worksheets, enlarge any particularly dense text and then gradually reduce the size of the print as the student's reading speed increases.
- Encourage the students to practise reading quickly on a regular basis and to record their progress. It is easy to drift back into slow reading unless a conscious effort is made.
- When reading, the student should ensure the environment is as quiet as possible and distractions kept to a minimum.
- Stress the need for concentration. It is essential to focus in order to increase reading speed. Give the reader a set period of time for reading, then stop and check their understanding. When reading time is limited, the reader will realise they must pay attention to the material, but only for a short while. Gradually extend the period of time. If the reader keeps a notepad handy, they can jot down any distracting thoughts to return to later and get back to their reading.
- When reading longer pieces of text, teach the students to read the introduction and summary, but flick over the detail in the middle. This will give an overview of the information rather than allowing them to get bogged down and confused by irrelevant detail and padding. Students should only read the middle section if it seems relevant. Focus on meaningful keywords rather than connectives. The first sentence in the paragraph will give the main idea of the passage and subsequent text give examples or explanation. Teach the student to focus on understanding the main points.

Chapter 4

Whole school reading events

This chapter discusses ways to:

- increase student motivation
- hold successful reading events
- strengthen home–school links
- raise the profile of the school library
- promote reading in the form room
- organise whole school initiatives.

Increase student motivation

Increasing motivation must be a major focus when working with older reluctant readers. The majority of students with weaker skills do not need a specialist programme, extra phonic input or a graded reading scheme, they just need to be encouraged to read, persuaded they can read and have reading presented as a purposeful and pleasurable activity.

It might be assumed that the point at which an individual begins to read is when they start school and learn sound-to-symbol correspondence. However, the foundations for reading are laid before the child enters school on those occasions when they first come across books and the written word. Perhaps family members have read to them, they have received books as presents, looked at comics in a doctor's waiting room or listened to stories at the Library, nursery or playgroup. This type of reading precedes the acquisition of decoding skills. The child realises that pages are turned sequentially, illustrations match the action described by the written text and that the words are read aloud in a predefined sequence in order to tell a story. Such early experiences are the times when reading is presented as a pleasurable activity and a positive attitude towards books established. A bedtime story from a close relative will always provide emotional reassurance and pleasure for the young child. Each individual will have different early experiences; some will have had extensive exposure to books, while other children's experience of reading will have been minimal.

Some older students may have enjoyed books initially and be competent readers, but have lost interest in reading as they have moved into secondary school. Other readers who have struggled to develop literacy skills may have turned to activities in which they experience more success; as they have grown older, it will become embarrassing for them to admit to any sort of reading problem and easier to dismiss reading as being boring. Every time they are asked to do a reading task and find it difficult, their negative attitude will be reinforced. Skills will only improve with practice, so it is vital that students are given a reason to read and a wealth of opportunities to develop their reading in motivating and non-threatening ways. Success will breed success: if students are able to read more effectively and with greater understanding, they will become increasingly aware of how useful reading can be. It is important for students to appreciate that reading is not an activity that just happens in school, but that it is an essential life skill.

Support strategies would include the following:

- **Short courses** to promote generic reading skills for all students during PHSE lessons or rolling study skills programmes. Such courses could form part of the PHSE programme for each year group. It is essential to raise levels of competency before tackling student motivation: it is difficult for anyone to enjoy an activity when they do not feel confident about their ability.
- **Students who find reading a chore** may have been asked to read books beyond their capability and, if reading holds little inherent interest for them, the whole activity will have seemed pointless. They will need to be redirected to more appropriate, meaningful material. Having a discussion with the student will be the starting point. Find out how much they read, what sort of material they enjoy, what topics interest them, whether they have books at home, if they go to the Library, use electronic reading devices or browse the internet. Do they read Hi-Fi, music or fashion magazines, car manuals, cookery books, annuals, comics or football programmes? A relaxed approach starting from individual interest can be a welcome relief for the student who may have been bombarded with specialist remedial programmes in the past. Commercial reading schemes may concentrate more on decoding than on reading for pleasure or on teaching students *how* to read.
- **Reading aloud** to students continues to be a worthwhile activity throughout their school career. Listening is a skill that may need development; some secondary-aged students will find it difficult to listen for any period of time. The attention span of such students may be extended if they are allowed to draw, design, or doodle whilst listening.
- The adult will need to **choose the text carefully** to ensure maximum interest. Any text will need to be entertaining, to the point, with action that is not too drawn out and descriptive passages limited. The adult will need to be familiar with the text, so they can add pace and expression when appropriate to maximise the students' attention. Approaches to extend, challenge and introduce readers to good literature will come later.
- When reading with students, **allow choice of material**. All reading is good. It is unnecessary to direct the student towards 'worthy' material, but better to respect their preferences and start from their personal interests.
- **Many students imagine fiction books** to be the only 'proper' books. An introduction to other texts and confirmation of their importance as reading material can be a revelation: magazines, websites, e-books, newspaper articles, poetry, manuals, graphic novels, short stories, comics and puzzle books would all fall into this category.
- **Books designed specifically for weaker readers** of secondary age can make assumptions about gender, social class and interests. Older students may not want to read reading age appropriate books if they appear condescending or removed from their own life experience. Secondary students want material that appears suitable for their age, the sort of books that their peers are accessing. One solution would be to use material designed for EAL (English as an Additional Language) students. There are a huge variety of books produced specifically for this group that are perfect for secondary-aged students with lower reading ages. EAL students may experience similar problems when reading, but for different reasons. Readers include abridged versions of the classics and exam set texts: *Sense and Sensibility*, *David Copperfield*, *To Kill a Mockingbird*, *Emma*, *The Diary of Anne Frank*, *Jane Eyre*, *Wind in the Willows*, *The Phantom of the Opera*, *The Stories of Sherlock Holmes*, *Oliver Twist*, *Bleak House*, *War of the Worlds*, *The Boy in the Striped Pyjamas*, *A Christmas Carol*, *Moby Dick*, *White Fang*, *Elephant Man*, *The 39 Steps* and *The Silver Sword*. Publications include non-fiction material such as the autobiographies of historical figures: Grace Darling, The Wives of Henry VIII, William Shakespeare, the Bronte Sisters, David Beckham and Nelson Mandela. There are plays, both collections of simple, short plays as well as abridged versions of traditional works: *Macbeth*, *Othello*, *Romeo and Juliet*, *A Midsummer's Night's Dream*, *My Fair Lady*. The language used in the books is simplified, the sentences comparatively short with texts graded

for reading level. While the texts are significantly shorter than the originals, they look like 'proper' paperbacks with adult titles and layout. The books are an ideal way into set texts as they give an overview of the material without any confusing padding, introducing students to the different characters, sequence of events and plot. The publishers produce worksheets with activities for follow up work, as well as providing suggestions for activities after each chapter or section in the book. Most of the books have accompanying CDs, enabling the reader to either listen as the text is read, or listen and follow the script in the book. There will be books simple and short enough to guarantee success for any less fluent reader.

- Sometimes an **introduction to a specific author** or series of books can be motivating. If an adult or good reader reads sections of a text aloud, students may become interested enough to read on either by themselves or sharing the reading with others. One aim when engaging students with books that interest them is to increase their reading stamina. Books are written as a whole and students will benefit most when they read the complete text, sometimes this is best achieved through paired or shared reading.
- **Reading extracts** from books that relate to mainstream subjects can provide an additional perspective to a topic, for example: *The Iron Man* by Ted Hughes for Science, *The Diary of Anne Frank*, *Goodnight Mr Tom*, *The War Horse* or *The Boy in the Striped Pyjamas* adding a human dimension to History modules. Everyone enjoys a good story.
- **Watching DVDs** of set texts will give an overview of the story as well as useful repetition of the names of characters and places for those who have a difficulty with pronunciation. Subtitles at the bottom of the screen provide additional, and often amusing, opportunities to follow text.
- Take the students to see **productions of plays**. Studying the language of a play in class can be a similar experience to reading a musical score, but never hearing the work played. The performance of a play is certain to bring increased understanding and recall.
- **Comic book** or Manga versions of set texts can give some students valuable visual input as well as being an acceptable alternative in the eyes of their peers.
- **Reading on websites** like Wattpad encourages students to read and write. They can see the sort of issues that interest their peer group and that they like to write about, helping reading to become more personal.
- **Collections of short stories** can appeal to readers with poor reading stamina. Many stories are short enough to be read in one sitting and condensed enough for the reader with a memory weakness to assimilate without the need for recap.
- **Poetry and rhyme** have always been popular with pupils and the simplicity and rhythm of prose will be attractive to the less fluent, older reader. Raps, choral reading and the lyrics of songs are certain to be of interest to older students, with karaoke providing an original and unobtrusive reading opportunity.
- **Reading plays aloud** in groups will improve confidence and fluency. There are many selections of plays published for reluctant older readers. Such plays are written to ensure each student has enough to read to maintain concentration and, because the reading is composed of short, easily managed sentences, give students time to glance ahead and prepare their next input. Most publishers produce comedies which may hold more appeal to some teenagers.
- **Reassure students** that it is acceptable to pick up a book and not read past the first few pages if it holds no intrinsic appeal. Negative perceptions are likely to be reinforced when a student feels they must plough on with something they are not enjoying. Students need to feel able to choose independently rather than have material forced on them.
- **Fun is an essential aspect of motivation**. Providing a wealth of reading material will help: novels, biographies, comics, short stories, magazines, brochures, guide books, instruction manuals and non-fiction books. Newspaper articles about interesting topics or articles of general interest: art, music, sport, films, fashion and current affairs. There will be a magazine or journal relating to every possible interest a student could have. Such material can be

browsed and dipped into: the students do not need to read the material sequentially from beginning to end. As the aim is to motivate, it is of no importance whether the newspaper is a broadsheet or a tabloid or whether the chosen comic will provide opportunities for higher order reading development.

- **Encourage alternative forms of reading** using IT: iPods, kindles, books online, downloads, e-readers and CDs. Some students may perceived this type of reading activity to be more adult.
- **Use students' current interests** and topical concerns: films, TV programmes, international sporting events or music festivals. It is possible to develop knowledge about any topic of personal interest through reading.
- **Many students prefer television to books**, so try to find material that links to television programmes, perhaps related articles in magazines or newspapers, autobiographies of celebrities or non-fiction books that are published as a follow up to popular TV programmes.
- **Associations** such as the United Kingdom Literacy Association, the Schools Library Association and the National Literacy Trust are excellent sources of information and resources relating to the promotion of reading across the secondary age group.
- **Newspapers** – see Advice Sheet 12 in Chapter 6 for more about using newspapers.

Hold reading events

'One off' events provide novel ways to raise the profile of reading within a school.

Suggestions for one-off reading events

Authors' visits

Information sites about authors and illustrators are accessible via the internet (www.nawe.co.uk or www.ContactAnAuthor.co.uk). Many authors are happy to come into schools to discuss their work and hold reading workshops. Once a personal contact has been established, students may be motivated by the idea of reading other books by the same author.

A book club

Establish a Student Book Group that meets once a month to discuss chosen texts. When students talk together about books, they are able to make sense of their responses to the text in the light of their peers' feedback. Other students' ideas will help the reader to extend or modify their own interpretations. The selected magazine, book or website should reflect student choice rather than teacher imposition. It may be a good idea to check that the material is available to download from a website like 'Listening Books', in order to ensure that it is accessible for all.

Personal recommendation

Have regular slots in Assemblies or Form Periods when members of staff or students read extracts or give short talks about books they have enjoyed.

Mount displays

Set up displays of book recommendations, other work by the same author, books in the same genre, or fiction and non-fiction material on the same topic. Advertise 'Good reads for artists/mathematicians/geographers/scientists.'

Hold book sales

Students, parents and staff can donate books and magazines they have finished, in addition to surplus stock from the Library.

Readathons

Hold Readathons and sponsored reading events to support a charity of the students' choice. Fund raising gives the more reluctant student a valid reason to read. The reading material does not have to be seen as intellectually worthy because the emphasis is on raising money for charity. Students could record reading comics, magazines, newspapers or easier books to younger siblings and students in other year groups.

Shadow book competitions

Organise the shadowing of book competitions such as the Carnegie Medal, the Costa Book of the Year and the Kate Greenaway Medal.

Read to the community

Students could go out of school on 'Reading Trips', perhaps reading books to children at the local nursery, or newspaper and magazine articles to residents at Old People's Homes, or patients in the local hospital.

Support World Book Day

The World Book Day website is an excellent resource for information and materials relating to the promotion of reading in schools.

Theatre and cinema trips

Organise theatre or cinema trips to see productions or films of set books and popular texts: *Matilda, War Horse, The 39 Steps, Romeo and Juliet, The Woman in Black, Les Misérables, Billy Elliot, The Wind in the Willows* and *The Curious Incident of the Dog in the Night*.

Associations and organisations

Contact associations and organisations interested in promoting reading among young people, such as:

- First Story
- The Literacy Shed
- Wattpad
- The Reading Agency
- Book Trust
- Film Club
- The School Library Association.

Strengthen home–school links

Events to encourage parents to support their children's reading will have to be organised within the context of each school and the families of pupils at that school. Some parents will experience problems that are more pressing than their child's reading levels. Individual schools will know

> Parents play a vital role in encouraging and supporting their children with reading.

how to best approach their parents and carers. Some parents will be happy to come into school for an evening meeting, others with younger children may prefer to meet in the afternoon, while some parents may not want to come into school and prefer to meet in a Community Centre, Church Hall or Sports Centre. Other parents may be unable to come to meetings because of work or family commitments, but appreciate an advice pamphlet. Some parents would come to an information session if it was part of a social event; others might come to a meeting at the end of the school day if a crèche was provided for younger children. The school will need to be flexible and offer a variety of alternatives.

Always offer parents the opportunity to become members of the school library, with a section of the Library stocking reading material specifically for this group.

It is useful to include information about reading in New Parents' packs or at New Parents' Induction Evenings. Such information needs to be provided in a clear, succinct style and give practical, realistic ideas about supporting readers. All information needs to be user friendly and any unfamiliar educational jargon avoided. The National Literacy Trust estimates that 20 per cent of the adult population in the UK experience problems with reading and it is likely that children with below average literacy levels will have parents with similar difficulties. However, as research shows that parental support contributes significantly to all areas of children's development, it is essential to pursue all possible avenues to involve parents. Some will be very zealous, others may have had a negative experience at school and be easily deterred if any proposed input appears complicated or beyond their capabilities. Support suggestions in a parental advice booklet will require sensitivity; some parents may work nights and not be available to help their children in the evening or may be single parents with children of different ages to get to bed.

Suggestions for possible points for inclusion in a parental advice sheet

- Let your child see you reading: magazines, newspapers, catalogues, pamphlets, recipes, websites, emails, instruction manuals, timetables, TV guides, and holiday brochures. The material doesn't have to be a book, but anything that will make it obvious that reading is a useful skill for adult life.
- Involve the children when you are reading for real purposes: 'to do' lists, emails, internet shopping, and when writing notes or reminders to yourself.
- When you read newspapers or magazines, point out interesting articles and information.
- Give books, comics or magazines as presents or treats. Encourage the children to discuss and exchange books and comics with their friends.
- Visit the Library and take out books, DVDs, magazines and CDs.
- Browse book stalls at jumble sales and look around second hand bookshops to find books that you think might interest your child.
- Be aware of any special reading events, promotions or competitions at the Library or local bookshop and encourage the children to attend or enter.
- Continue reading at bedtime for as long as possible: perhaps one chapter per night from a book, an interesting article from a magazine or support with reading homework. Albert Einstein once said, 'If you want your children to be intelligent, read them fairytales. If you want them to be more intelligent, read them more fairytales.'
- Visit bookshops regularly and browse. Direct the children towards non-fiction books: fashion, travel, pets, cinema, sport, careers, cars, music, computers, celebrities and politics. The text in non-fiction material tends to be chunked with a lot of the information presented visually and may be more appealing to some children.

- Encourage the children to be curious and use the internet to research information. Discuss interesting websites. When they ask you a question, look up the answer rather than say you don't know.
- Be aware of books linked to films or TV programmes that are popular with teenagers: *Doctor Who, War Horse, Star Trek, Tales of Narnia, Lord of the Rings, Shrek, The Hunger Games, Charlie and the Chocolate Factory, Charlotte's Web, Sherlock Holmes, Matilda, Harry Potter, The Twilight* series.
- Sometimes a child will enjoy a series of books after they have read one from a set, for example, the *Horrible Histories* or the *Twilight* or *Hunger Games* series.
- Fiction CDs can be a useful way to develop reading stamina if your child finds it difficult to read for long periods of time. CDs can be borrowed from the school or public library and can be listened to on the bus, in the car, the bath or before going to bed.

Raising the profile of the school library

- Ensure that the school library is accessible and welcoming to all. That it is open during lunch time, lesson breaks and after school and that all different resources are clearly signposted.
- Students and Teaching Assistants could take part in the running of the Library and support any extended opening hours.
- Let students take books home over holiday periods.
- Give student librarians responsibility for producing a regular library newsletter for their peers.
- Give student librarians responsibilities, for example, creating suggestions lists in the style of, 'If you liked this, try...'.
- Display suitable fiction lists for 'reading around' subjects, lists of reading material for specific topics and collaborate with mainstream staff over topic-based research. Display these lists in subject classrooms and ask students which of the books they have read and would recommend.
- Promote specific books and general Library resources on the school intranet or as screen savers.
- Quiet corners of the Library are the perfect place for one-to-one or small group reading sessions. If volunteers come into school to hear readers, they can be supported by the Librarian within an environment considered safe in terms of child protection. The presence of this type of industrious activity will ensure the Library is perceived as being a popular and purposeful work area.
- Have regular competitions and reading challenges with prizes and feedback. Match the teacher to their favourite book: in which book would you be able to read these famous quotes, match the first line to the book or which of these characters appear in which novel?
- Shadow book awards and see how student recommendation compares with the national results.
- Hold 'Introduction to the Library' sessions for all students at the beginning of each school year to remind them of the layout of the Library, opening times, how books are stored, how to reserve books, how many books can be borrowed, where magazines and newspapers are kept and which magazines and newspapers are ordered regularly. Students need to understand how to access information both within a library and within books (index, references and contents pages). They may have been told before, but it is always worth reminding them to ensure that using the Library is as easy as possible.
- Hold special events for different year groups, perhaps to remind students in exam years of the revision resources kept in the Library, or study skills sessions for younger pupils.
- Display clear instructions about how to access Library iPods, kindles and computers.
- Give advice about how to choose books to read. Explain how to look at any illustrations, blurb, opening paragraphs and cover design to judge a book's appeal.
- Encourage students to form specialist reading groups: a Fighting Fantasy, Star Wars, Trading cards or Music Technology group.

- Have a 'Library promotion' slot at every Parents' Evening with a display of material and resources from the Library. A local bookseller might be happy to manage such a stand and suggest suitable reading material for specific age ranges.
- Mainstream teaching staff should regularly examine the range of resources the Library stocks for their subject and recommend new or updated material to the Librarian. This may be particularly necessary for extension reading material for 'A/S' and 'A' Level students.
- Silent reading lessons in the Library are a questionable use of time during which an unknown number of students may be engaged with their texts. While enthusiastic readers may enjoy the opportunity to engage with their current reading material, weaker readers will be aware of the level of text they are able to read and be tempted to choose something too difficult in order to match the choices of their peers. It will be more useful to set tasks or devise games and challenges that involve research and reading for a purpose.
- Parents could be encouraged to buy a book for the Library when their child leaves the school.
- Books do not have to be new; second hand bookshops and public libraries will sell appropriate material for reduced prices.
- Hold story telling sessions at lunch times and breaks: ghost and horror stories read in atmospheric conditions may appeal to some students.
- If you suspect certain students read very little or choose books aimed at a younger audience, it may be worth directing them towards CD versions of books for older readers so they can gain access to age appropriate vocabulary.
- Work with statistical evidence. What material is borrowed most frequently? By which groups? Track individual student's use of the Library. Do reading patterns have implications for future purchases or subscriptions?
- Have regular surveys to ask pupils what sort of reading material they would like the Library to stock.
- Ensure a balance of genders and ages are seen using and working in the Library: male teachers, governors, lunch time supervisors, reading mentors, sixth formers and outside speakers.
- Invite authors into school to speak about their work. Hold competitions that relate to their talks: design an alternative book cover, finish a story in a different way, write a story in the same genre or describe what has happened to the characters in 20 years time. Ask the author to judge the competition and distribute prizes.
- Liaise and establish links with librarians in other schools for the sharing of ideas.
- Liaise and establish links with local bookshops: they may be happy to come into school to talk to the students or for students to go to the bookshop for talks about reading material.
- Liaise and establish links with the local public library.
    - Are specialist collections available for schools to borrow?
    - Are staff willing to show groups of students around the library and take time to show them the different types of resources they stock in addition to books?
    - Could local librarians be invited into school to talk to students about reading-related issues or to take Assemblies?

Suggestions for displays in the Library

- Student reviews of books and films of books.
- Displays of funny or insightful quotes from books.
- Displays of students' research findings about the historical or geographical settings of stories.
- Newspaper articles students have written based on incidents from books.
- Displays of adapted or simplified versions of stories designed for younger students, for example, the 'Cosy Classics' series.

- Poster adverts for books with space around the advert for written feedback or comments from readers.
- Biographies or obituary notices for the leading characters in stories using information gleaned from the reading.
- Mind maps to show the relationships of the characters from a story and interesting facts about each of them.
- Story maps to show plots, dates and settings.
- Newspaper headlines of 20 words or less summarising the content of a book.
- Letters students have written to authors explaining why they liked specific texts they had written.
- Comic strips to show the action of or a series of events in a story.
- Jacket designs for books, complete with illustrations and blurbs.
- Acrostics. Letter the title of the book vertically and write a sentence about the book for each letter.
- Lists of the kind of people who would enjoy this book and the kind who wouldn't.
- Ten questions about a text that a reader should be able to answer.
- Reviews of books for the literature section of a newspaper or magazine.
- Magazine articles based on a book for a publication such as *Country Life*, *OK* or *Rolling Stone*. What scenes from the book should be photographed? Supply captions and describe the photographs.
- Display books by particular authors, the author's biography and lists of all of their books with a résumé of the content, photos of the author and any publicity posters their publishers are able to supply.
- Displays that promote reading material, perhaps powerful extracts from fiction or questions that a non-fiction text would be able to answer. Different years, clubs, subject teachers and groups within the school could be given responsibility for this on a rotational basis.
- Change displays regularly: have a book of the week, an author of the week and student recommendations boards.
- Mount additional book displays around the school: in the Entrance Hall, staff room, sports hall, music room and dining area.

Promote reading in the form room

> The targeting of reading in subject lessons gives opportunities to promote non-fiction material.

- Keep an interest box of laminated cuttings and articles about subject topics in the classroom and read from them occasionally during lessons.
- Talk about books relating to your subject, those you have enjoyed reading in the past and any you are reading at the moment.
- Recommend magazines, websites and books relating to your subject.
- Share your enthusiasm for your subject or hobby by reading from magazine articles or newspaper extracts.
- Share recommendations from other readers: teachers, non-teaching staff, teachers from other schools, friends, parents, from bookshops or material reviewed on television or in newspapers.
- Provide book lists for topics studied in class.
- Take an interest in books the students are reading.
- Look up information about individual student's interests on the internet and print off articles for them to read.
- Have books, papers and magazines about your personal work area.
- Encourage students to collect articles, newspaper cuttings, brochures and leaflets that relate to your subject and to bring books into school about subject topics or modules from home.

- Mount wall displays about some of the most famous writers in your field: scientists, artists, sports personalities, musicians, chefs and historians.
- Display information about the important texts written on your subject.
- Display newspaper cuttings, magazine articles and internet features about modules students are studying currently.
- Have one new 'Word a Day/Week' that all the students are expected to learn. Encourage students to keep a notebook for the recording of interesting words.
- Have dictionaries and thesauruses on display and available in every classroom and demonstrate their less obvious uses, for example, how word listings include symbols to aid with the pronunciation of unfamiliar words. Using a dictionary may seem an old-fashioned way to look words up, but if the internet is not available, it can be useful prop.

Organising whole school initiatives

- Create a school website with personal recommendations for books: books of topical interest; books that are in the news at the moment; suggestions for books to be read by the time you are 14, 16 or 18; and 'If you liked this, you'll love this …'recommendations.
- Have a book review section on the school website. Update the reviews regularly.
- Collect books and magazines for Swap Boxes. Encourage students to bring in magazines, comics, journals or books they have read and are prepared to exchange. Organise a rota of students to update and tidy the boxes.
- Have displays of books in corridors, the entrance area, main halls, the dining room and classrooms.
- Display lists of interesting information websites linked to different topics.
- Mount displays of subject-related books in different subject bases, for example, biographies of music or sports personalities in the Music rooms and PE changing rooms.
- Mount displays relating to set texts in the relevant Year's classroom area: abridged texts, revision guides, manga and comic versions of the text, CDs to read alongside the original, reviews of theatre productions and posters of films or TV productions of the book.
- Display alternative sources of information about topics in corridors. If the current topic in Geography is Volcanoes, collect and display relevant newspaper and magazine articles, photographs, information about famous eruptions (Pompeii, Mount St Helens, Etna), and extracts from the Horrible History, Science and Geography series, a popular series of books presenting information about basic topics in cartoon form and of appeal to readers who enjoy reading information in a comic strip format.
- Hold Reading Assemblies where magazines, newspapers, online resources books are recommended by students from different year groups.
- Provide time for reading in class and for homework. Let students know that you will be asking questions about their reading and that 'reading homework' is not 'no homework', but a warm up for interesting discussions in class.
- Track individual students' reading habits and give rewards for reading. Organise within school reading qualifications with certificates, prizes and privileges given to participants.
- Run promotions for new Library stock in the school's entrance hall or reception areas.

Chapter 5

Stand alone reading lessons

This chapter contains sample lessons on how to:

- improve reading habits and reading techniques
- expand students' vocabulary
- boost general knowledge
- increase students' reading speed
- make progress with comprehension
- extend students' knowledge of subject vocabulary.

Lesson 1: Reading habits and reading techniques

Three sample lessons are provided in this section.

> The lessons or combinations of lessons, could be used for staff INSET to raise awareness of the many skills underlying reading.

Lesson 1(a)

Learning objective

Students will be aware of which aspects of their reading would benefit from an increased focus.

Resources required

Photocopied reading questionnaires for students.

Activities

Students fill in a brief questionnaire to initiate discussion about their reading habits.

Students' responses will give teaching staff an idea of the number of individuals who experience different types of problems and potential groupings for focused support.

Reading questionnaire

- Why do you think that people read? How many reasons can you think of?
- Do you read for pleasure? If so, when and for how long?
- What sort of reading material do you like? Fiction, non-fiction, web pages, magazines, comics, newspapers?
- Who are your favourite authors and why?
- What is your favourite book? Why does it appeal to you?
- Do you read magazines? If so, which ones do you choose?

- Does anything make reading hard for you? If so, what?
- Do you use the school and/or public library?
- What do you plan to do when you leave school or college? How useful will reading be for that type of job or career?

Speed

- Do you read slowly? Do you ever read so slowly that you find it hard to make sense of what you have read?
- Do you think you read slower than other students?

Comprehension

- Do you always understand everything you read?
- What do you do when you don't understand?
- Could you summarise in your own words the book you are reading currently in English lessons?

Decoding

- Do you ever have a problem working out the pronunciation of words that you haven't seen before?
- Do you enjoy reading aloud in class? If not, why?

Lesson 1(b)

Learning objective

Students will be able to differentiate between different reading techniques and identify the occasions when different techniques should be used.

Resources required

A selection of holiday brochures, magazines, timetables, newspapers and directories.

Activities

The teacher explains and models skimming and scanning techniques emphasising that there are a range of approaches to reading and it is not always necessary to read material carefully from beginning to end. It would be nonsensical to read all of a railway timetable to see at what time your train arrives, all of a sports page to see if your team had won a match or all of the phone book to find the number of a local taxi firm.

We **skim** read to get an overview of a text, perhaps the section on Christianity in an encyclopaedia to see if the information is relevant for a project. Skimming gives the feel of a text before the reader decides whether to read it in depth or to remind them of the content if they have read the text previously. Skimming would involve reading through the introductory paragraphs, any highlighted sections, headings, summaries and looking at illustrations. The teacher could demonstrate this by modelling how to skim a chapter from a class text.

We **scan** a text to look for specific information: a grandparent's grocery list to see if they need a jar of coffee or a calendar to confirm the date of a dental appointment. The subject teacher could model scanning by demonstrating how ineffective it would be to read a whole chapter from the class text to find one specific detail, but how to use an index, chapter headings and titles to target the search appropriately.

We **read closely** to check information thoroughly: a new mobile phone contract or a question in an exam paper to ensure understanding. Students need to be reminded to read complex sentences carefully: any sentences with brackets, colons and semi colons will need to be read section by section. The teacher could model this approach by reading a complex piece of information from a school textbook, breaking complex sentences down into their constituent parts and re-ordering the content if this helps understanding.

Discuss whether it would be sensible to skim, scan or read closely in a variety of situations:

- Looking up a train arrival time on a timetable.
- Reading a long and boring letter from your aunt.
- Reading instructions for a Maths test.
- Seeing when an interesting programme is on television.
- Looking at a gardening book to see if it would make a suitable present for your granddad.
- Looking for an item in a shopping list.
- Looking at a library book to see if it might be useful for a History project.
- The students could think of further examples where skimming, scanning or close reading would be appropriate techniques.

Use extracts taken from newspapers and magazines as practice for skimming. Ask the students to write text messages summarising the gist of newspaper reports and articles from magazines.

Use recipes, timetables, holiday brochures, telephone directories, TV programmes as material for scanning. Set the students ten questions, for example. At what time is the *Archers' Omnibus* programme? How much would a half-board holiday for four cost at the Madeira Hotel in the first week of September? What are the two main ingredient of Apple Fool? How long would it take to travel from Peterborough to Birmingham with a change at Leicester, if you caught the 8.45 am train from Peterborough? Time the students as they look up: a set number of addresses in the phone book, times of ten TV programmes, quotes about specific topics from a class textbook or the prices of six holidays from a brochure.

Lesson 1(c)

Learning objective

Students will be aware of the different approaches that may be necessary when reading non-fiction texts for meaning.

Resources required

Photocopied articles from magazines, newspapers or books.

Activities

The adult chooses two interesting pieces of text, for example, an article from a newspaper, magazine or book, preferably with one or two visual displays of information, perhaps a graph or illustration. The article should have content that will appeal to the age and interest of the students: Music, Fashion, Media, History, Politics, Sport, Animals, Art or Science. Model the approach the students are to take with the first text and let them work with a partner on the second piece of text following the same routine.

1. **Activate prior knowledge.** Ask the students to look at the title of the article and discuss with a partner what they already know about this topic, listing a few facts of interest. This will demonstrate how to 'tune in' to the topic: *'The article is about the outbreak of World War 1. I watched a film on TV last week about that with my Dad. Now, what can I remember? ...'*

2. **Skim the text.** The students then skim read any headings, charts, maps and pictures to get an idea of what the material will cover. This will narrow the reader's attention to the specific focus of the information: *'It seems to be about men volunteering to join the army when the war first started.'*
3. **Scan the text if appropriate.** Highlight any pertinent dates, names or numbers as required: *'I'll highlight any information about the numbers of men who joined the army in the first six months of the war and any relevant dates.'*
4. **Read the text aloud.** Highlight any unfamiliar words or concepts: *'What do the words "conscripts", "the front" and "enlistment" mean?'*
5. **Discuss the meaning of any unknown words.** Use suffixes, prefixes, word families and context to help: *'There's a bit here about eight new "conscripts" from one Welsh village travelling together to France, so conscripts probably means the men who have just joined the army.'*
6. **Summarise the main idea.** What is the article about? Music of the 1980s? Discrimination in Sport? The dangers of obesity? Alcoholism? New film releases? *'This is mainly about how enthusiastic men were to go and fight in the war.'*
7. **Identify any supporting details.** Look for any further information that will expand, support and clarify the main points: *'There's a bit here about a fifteen-year-old boy who joined up because he was frightened that the war would be over before he was really old enough to fight. Everyone told him the war would be over soon and he didn't want to miss it.'*
8. **Ask the students to represent the main idea and supporting information in an alternative format.** Perhaps a timeline, concept map, mind map, pie chart, comic strip or a linear list: *'I could put all of this information about patterns of enlistment into a timeline for the first six months. I imagine that enlistment decreased as the war went on. I wonder if that is true?'*

It may be enlightening to ask students how they would judge their current subject texts. This will help them to evaluate objectively what is helpful in a non-fiction book. The subject teacher could use this feedback when preparing worksheets or selecting new textbooks.

- Do you think the format of this text is helpful for students?
- Is the content well organised and clearly set out?
- Do books in this subject tend to be easy or difficult to read? Why do you think this might be?
- How much information is given visually? Do you find visual information helpful?
- Does the text link to what you already know about this topic?
- Have you used other textbooks for this subject that you have preferred? Why were they preferable?
- Does this book make you want to learn more about the subject?

Lesson 2: Generic vocabulary

The difference in the language experience of children is well documented: some Year 3 children will have a vocabulary of 7,000 words and others 3,000 words. Pupils will need a vocabulary of 9,000 words in order to cope successfully with the secondary curriculum, with 18- year-olds in full-time education possessing a vocabulary of between 12, 000 and 18,000 words. The majority of university graduates have a vocabulary of between 18,000 and 24,000 words, while 25 per cent of the adult population have a vocabulary of between only 6,000 and 12,000 words.

> Knowledge of vocabulary is not linked to innate ability, but to home–school experience.

The specific learning difficulties that affect a student's performance occur on a spectrum and sometimes even a specialist teacher can be uncertain of the root of a student's difficulties. Is the problem of a limited vocabulary the result of a specific language difficulty, developmental delay, because the pupil does not read for pleasure or as a result of inadequate language input in the pupil's childhood?

The positive correlation between vocabulary and academic success make the acquisition of language a key educational issue. If students are to achieve academically, it will be essential for them to develop their knowledge base. If students are able to understand the words they read, they will be free to concentrate on the overall meaning of the text. An inadequate vocabulary will limit reading competence and comprehension and yet it is easy for a teacher to assume a student can understand a text just because they are able to decode the words.

Some students will direct all of their energy into working out the correct pronunciation of words. This is common amongst weak readers when reading in front of their peers; all of their effort will be focused on decoding the words accurately and avoiding embarrassment, but leaving little focus for understanding.

As students move through school it is possible for them to appear articulate, but only to be using conversational vocabulary and have little comprehension of the formal language of texts. This will put them at a disadvantage in secondary school and further or higher education. There is a need to think in increasingly abstract terms as students progress through school and a good vocabulary is essential for the development of abstract thought. If a student has a developed vocabulary, they will find it easier to maintain concentration, to follow arguments and understand information.

The most effective way for individuals to increase their general vocabulary is through reading. The more a student reads, the more extensive their vocabulary will become, giving them a distinct advantage in academic settings.

Lesson 2(a)

Learning objective

The students will appreciate the importance of developing and extending their vocabulary.

Resources required

- Extracts from a KS1, KS4 and/or A Level texts.
- Whiteboard or OHP.

Activities

Introduce the topic by pointing out that it is vital for individuals to continue to develop their vocabulary throughout life. By way of a demonstration, ask one student to read an extract from a Key Stage 1 reading book aloud and then a second, (more confident reader), to read aloud from an 'A' Level or postgraduate text. It will be obvious that students have made great developmental strides already, but that this development needs to continue.

KS1 text:

> So the people shouted and shouted and shouted. They said, 'Get out of the way.
>
> They wanted to get to important places. The dog didn't want to get out of the way.

'A' Level text:

> A two-variable linear programming problem can be solved graphically. The strategy is to plot lines representing the equality case for each constraint and then shade the region where the

inequality is not satisfied. The region that is never shaded is the feasible region where all the constraints are satisfied.

Vocabulary can be divided into four groups:

1. **Conversational words**: she, aloud, horse, feet. Students will be most comfortable when working within this group.
2. **Academic words**: initiate, perspective, conclusion, advanced. These are words that will need to be taught directly.
3. **Technical words**: schwa, consonant, tectonic, environment. These are words that will need to be taught directly.
4. **Rare words**: elision, imbost, bruxomania. These are words that students will come across when they read about specialist topics and so are not necessary as a focus.

Write a list of words on the board, choosing some words that students will use in conversation and others that they are more likely to come across in written text. Ask the students to identify those words they would use and put them into one column, those words they understand, but would not use into a second column, and those words they have not met in a third column. A list that might be appropriate for Key Stage 3 might be: sport, classrooms, duration, epicure, summary, blithe, bulwark, podium, shouting, tenuous, short, rescind and important. This will show that it is always possible to continue to learn new words and extend one's vocabulary. When working on vocabulary, it is most useful to focus on the words that:

- The student recognises, but would not feel confident enough to use in oral or written work and attempt to move such words from their column 2 to their column 1 (*Generic vocabulary*).
- The student needs to know for everyday use in secondary school, FE and HE. These will be the academic and technical words that need to be taught *directly* in order for the student to progress through levels of difficulty within subjects (*Subject specific vocabulary*).

Additional activities

1. **Play 'Call my Bluff'** in teams of three. Each group finds a word in the dictionary that they think will be unfamiliar to other students and record the word's definition. The group then make up two incorrect definitions for the word and present the three definitions to the rest of the class. The class have to guess which of the three definitions is correct.
2. **Research idioms.** Idioms are words, phrases, or expressions that cannot be taken literally. When used in everyday language, they have a meaning other than the one found in a dictionary. For example, 'break a leg' is a common idiom. The literal meaning would be I'm telling you to break a bone in your leg. The idiomatic meaning would be to do your best and good luck. Actors are believed to use this expression to encourage others in the cast before they go on stage. The ability to make sense of idioms and other sayings may cause some individuals problems. 'Pull the plug', 'Ants in your pants', 'You're going to have to pull your socks up' all could be interpreted literally. However, these sayings occur so frequently in written texts that it is useful to explore the more common ones.

    Students could make collections of idioms relating to one specific word, for example, 'break': 'You are going to break my heart'; 'Be careful, you will break your neck'; 'It is difficult to break the ice at a party', or design an illustration of a popular saying to show how illogical some of the idioms we use every day could sound to others. Any aspect of English that presents a problem for a non-English speaker will give students with a language weakness similar difficulties. For example:

- *A friend in need is a friend indeed.* A real friend is around when you need them.
- *An own goal.* To do something that counts against you.
- *Any port in a storm.* To get out of danger in any way possible.
- *A stitch in time saves nine.* To do something as soon as it is necessary will save you having to do more work later.
- *A fair-weather friend.* A person who is a friend during the good times, but not when things get difficult.
- *Adding fuel to the fire.* Aggravating a situation.
- *A piece of cake.* Something that is easily done.
- *Working against the clock.* Working to a deadline.
- *All bark and no bite.* To talk more aggressively but not follow through with action.
- *A herd of elephants.* Noisy, unsubtle, obvious.

3. **Research proverbs.** A proverb is a succinct saying that offers some practical advice. Discussing proverbs with students will help them to understand inference or reading between the lines. Here are some examples:

   - *Don't make a mountain out of a molehill* = Do not exaggerate the size of the problem.
   - *Easier said than done* = It is easier to talk about doing something than actually perform the task.
   - *A cat may look at a king* = Even the lowliest have rights.
   - *Every man has his price* = Everyone is open to bribery if the inducement is sufficient.
   - *One swallow does not a summer make* = A single indicator is not in itself significant.
   - *Live and let live* = Show the tolerance towards others that you would like them to show you.
   - *Every cloud has a silver lining* = There is always reason for hope, even in the most desperate circumstances.
   - *No news is good news* = Without information to the contrary, it is best to assume that all is well.
   - *Revenge is sweet* = Getting one's own back is satisfying.
   - *Don't hide your light under a bushel* = Do not hide your talents through modesty or shyness.

   Students could see how many proverbs they can find relating to one topic. Animals: A bird in the hand is worth two in the bush. Curiosity killed the cat. The early bird catches the worm. Let sleeping dogs lie.

4. **Look closely at *synonyms* and *antonyms*.** Ask the students to write out their own lists of synonyms putting one decoy word in the list. Their partner then has to spot the odd one out, for example, definite, certain, indisputable, doubtful, sure.

5. **Play games with dictionaries and thesauruses** as appropriate to the student's age and level of understanding and have question and answer sessions using the dictionary. Students can make up quizzes of five questions for the rest of the class. Why would a farmer leave a field fallow? What part of a dog is its muzzle? What does an optometrist do? If we lament, are we sad or happy?

6. **Use the internet to research the origins of words.** English vocabulary includes many words from other countries: major, orange, yacht, dinosaur, bungalow, cosh, wagon, aloof and shampoo.

7. **Compare similarities between languages:** mother, maman and mutter. Address, adresse and addresse.

8. **Collect homonyms.** Demonstrate that the pronunciation of homonyms will depend on context, for example:

   - bow – a wooden stick with horse hair that is used to play certain string instruments
   - bow – to bend forward at the waist as a mark of respect
   - bow – the front section of a ship

- bow – a kind of tied ribbon
- bow – to bend outward at the sides
- Bow – a district in London

9. **Ask the students to keep a diary for a week.** Each day they jot down five new words they hear that are unfamiliar. At the end of the week, they compare their lists and see if they know words from their peers' lists well enough to put into sentences.

10. **Have short, fun vocabulary activities** as input to introductory or plenary sessions. Choose from the activities, as appropriate to the age and ability of the group.

    - How many compound words can be listed in two minutes: tailgate, birdcage, haircut, eggcup, and netball?
    - Write a short passage that includes a few specified words: ousted, feeble, lethargy, isolated and perplexed. 'The lethargy of the old, feeble wolf isolated him from his perplexed family, and they ousted him from the pack'.
    - Students design a quiz for different letters of the alphabet to test their peers. The clue must be a synonym. To supply = p------. To creep = p----. Strange = p--------.
    - Find the male equivalent of female words: nephew and niece, stallion and mare, maternal and paternal.
    - Give the students a list of sentences where one word is used repeatedly. Replace the word with more descriptive words. Walk could be changed to stumbled, ambled, strolled, marched, hobbled or sauntered.
    - Make adjectives from nouns and nouns from adjectives: distant/distance, silk/silky, wise/wisdom.
    - Collect group terms: a swarm of bees, a litter of puppies, a bouquet of flowers, a pride of lions, and a troupe of dancers.
    - Guess the definitions of nonsense words from a passage using context and grammatical knowledge.
    - Give the students copies of material they wouldn't normally read (gardening books, deep sea fishing information, sailing manuals or golfing magazines), and show them how to work out the meanings of unfamiliar words.
    - Quizzes to be completed in two minutes. List as many types of dog, tree, colour, minerals, insects, sport, flower, and occupations beginning with the letter 's' as you can. List as many words related to: the coast, volcanoes, magnetism or electricity as you can. List as many technical historical, biological, geographical words as you can that begin with 'r' in one minute.
    - Discuss how to work out the meanings of words using *prefixes* and *suffixes*. For example: em = from, im = into, -ant = one who. Collections of words can be written on the board, and their meanings deduced by the students using prior knowledge and knowledge of the parts of words. Emigrate, emigration, immigrant, migrant, immigrate and migratory. Act, action, proactive, inactive, reactive and activity. Telephone, television, telegraph and telescope.

11. Play games with dictionaries and thesauruses as appropriate to the student's age and level of understanding.

    - Play 'Connections'. Start with a word from the dictionary. Each pair or group has to guess another word that will appear in the dictionary as a definition for that word. For example the word 'seek' will appear as an alternative to the word 'search'. The students then guess a word that will appear as an alternative to seek. The winners are the group able to make the longest unbroken chain of slightly different words.
    - Time the students as they look up a specified number of words in the dictionary. Record their individual times to show how competence increases with practice.

- Dramatise moods: fear, boredom, despair, contempt, pain, wonder, hope, reluctance, rage, generosity, pity, admiration, joy, reverence, hate, jealousy, love, anticipation, loneliness, envy, compassion, impatience, satisfaction, resentment, pride, disgust, doubt, contentment, shame, surprise greed, discontentment, repentance, gratitude, anxiety and resignation.
- Look up the meanings of confusable words, and clarify their definitions with cartoons, drawings or mnemonics: currant and current, adverse and averse, illegible and ineligible, empathic and empathise.
- Research the origins of words. *Specta* is Latin for to look, hence our words: spectator, respectable, spectacles, inspect and prospect.
- Examine well-known old English texts: *The Pilgrim's Progress*, Shakespeare's plays or *The Canterbury Tales*, for vocabulary and words that reflected fashionable society of the time. Work out their modern day equivalent.

Teaching strategies: vocabulary

- Encourage wide reading as a way to extend vocabulary.
- Give direct instruction about the meanings of words.
- Demonstrate ways to record and learn vocabulary.
- Read passages of text aloud in class to assist with correct pronunciation and give opportunities to explain the meanings of words.
- Show students how to look up words using printed or online dictionaries and thesauruses.
- Teach prefixes, suffixes and root words to help students work out the meanings of unfamiliar words.
- Link reading, pronunciation and spelling.
- Display curiosity yourself about words, their origins, meanings and correct spelling.

Student advice sheet: how to learn new words

- Look carefully at the word and think about how it might be pronounced.
- Examine the context of the sentence to see if it is possible to work out the word's meaning.
- Look for any prefixes, suffixes or roots in the word.
- Make a guess and read on to see if your guess would make sense in the context of the passage.
- Look up the word in a printed or online dictionary or in a textbook glossary.
- If you think you almost understand the word or if doesn't seem important in the passage, read on. No one always understands every word they come across.

Lesson 3: General knowledge

Some teaching staff assume a level of general knowledge that students do not possess. Adequate comprehension of more complex material will depend on a good vocabulary, an appreciation of the grammatical structure of the text and adequate background knowledge.

> When the system is exposed to molecules that are foreign to the body, it will orchestrate an immune response, developing the ability to respond to a subsequent encounter because of immunological memory.

Even when the reader can decode this passage, unless they have some understanding of the process of vaccination and are familiar with the specialist vocabulary used in the sentence, the text will make little sense. The teacher may not realise this. The problem of teachers making assumptions about background knowledge can present difficulties for students throughout their academic careers.

A reasonable general knowledge is essential before a student can understand any text as any gaps in knowledge will give problems at a very basic level. The sentence, 'the cat sat on the mat', would prove difficult to understand if a reader was uncertain of what a cat or a mat was and how the domesticated cat tends to live in the family home.

General knowledge will become increasingly important when the focus of reading moves from decoding to reading for understanding. The frequency, extent and level at which gaps in background knowledge occur are not always appreciated by the teacher, who may assume that information is obvious because they are familiar with it themselves.

The confusions for the reader will be similar to those experienced by EAL (English as an Additional Language) students when texts are based on culturally specific topics. The reader can have a difficulty in all subjects, even Science and Maths which might be assumed to be non-language specific. Difficulties may arise when questions are couched in language to make problems seem more interesting and relevant to real life. In a question such as, 'How many holiday makers can twelve six-berth caravans accommodate?', the actual calculation is simple, but the EAL reader may wonder who is making the holiday, who is giving birth, what the word 'accommodate' means and what a caravan is. They will be flummoxed by the question even though they are capable of doing the required calculations.

One of the main ways that general knowledge can be extended is by reading, so once again the weak reader is placed at a disadvantage. When students can be persuaded to read non-fiction texts, they will acquire useful information and get overviews of a wide range of topics.

It is always necessary when introducing a new module or information to check students' prior knowledge and not to show surprise if they reveal how little they know about a topic. When students are encouraged to ask questions in lessons without ridicule or reprimand, they are more likely to try to clarify areas of uncertainty. Poor reading skills will make the likelihood of an individual reading around a subject unlikely, increasing the likelihood of the student making their own sense of information and developing erroneous concepts. When these become embedded in the students' mental schema, further associated information will be built on the misunderstandings, however ridiculous they may appear to others. Elicitation of previous knowledge will give the teacher an insight into what background information needs to be explicitly taught. When links can be made with existing knowledge, new information will make sense to the student and deeper learning more likely to take place. If links are not made, the student will either not learn anything or be forced to remember isolated facts by rote.

Activation of prior knowledge can be done in several ways: Venn diagrams, concept maps, word webs, graphic organisers such as mind maps and class discussion. Discussion is particularly important. Students may mention films or television programmes they have watched that relate to the topic or discuss their personal experience, perhaps having seen examples of geographical features whilst on holiday or in their local area. The discussion will be in conversational language and therefore easier for other pupils to understand and use to fill in gaps in their own knowledge.

Lesson 3

Learning objective

Students will be aware of the importance of possessing an adequate general knowledge and how to develop their own background understanding.

Resources required

- Student access to the internet.
- Selection of newspaper articles.

Activities

1. Select and read newspaper articles that you know will be of interest to the students. Discuss the information in pairs or small groups in order to share any knowledge the students already have about the topic. When students hear the ideas of others and have the opportunity to talk about their own understanding, their personal knowledge will be extended. The language used during such informal discussions will be at the students' level and so information will be made more memorable.
2. Help the students to research information and encourage curiosity through modelling: 'I wonder why that is? Just a moment and I'll look it up and see when that happened'. Why are there five rings in the Olympic symbol? Why are the rings different colours? Why are they those colours? Who designed that symbol and when? Does anyone in the class know? Get students into the habit of finding answers rather than simply being curious and then moving on.
3. Use personal interests to develop general knowledge. If the reader supports West Ham Football Club, that interest could generate curiosity about the club's geographical whereabouts, the history of the club, the country of origin of any international players, how injuries affect players' performance, the cost of players and their salaries compared to other occupations.
4. Research general knowledge and information resources: magazines, comics, journals, websites, books and the internet.
5. Many publishers produce board and card games based on general knowledge, for example, the Brain Box or Brain Bites series. These games will quiz students on innumerable topics such as: The Tudors, flags of the world, capital cities, classical music, historical figures, scientific terms, animals and their habitats, Shakespearean plays, verbal reasoning and geographical features.
6. Play general knowledge games and quizzes. Organise inter-group/inter-class/inter-house Trivial Pursuits and 'Pub Quiz' type competitions.
7. Encourage the students to go to school clubs and societies, particularly when outside speakers are giving talks.

Lesson 4: Reading speed

Slow, careful reading is essential when reading complex text. However, some students will read silently at the same pace at which they read aloud. This lack of speed may deter them from reading for pleasure and will put them at a disadvantage as they move through secondary school and are expected to read increasing amounts of material.

It is possible to increase reading speed with regular practice. To maintain interest and confidence levels, encourage students to try to increase their reading speed *gradually*, rather than risk any early failure.

Practice will make perfect: give students opportunities to practise the techniques on all kinds of reading material in order to embed the approach.

Lesson 4(a)

Learning objective

Students will understand how and when to increase their reading speed.

Resources required

- A class reader or suitable fiction text.
- Rulers.
- Stopwatches.
- A selection of different coloured A4 plastic overlays.

Activities

1. Measure reading speed. Use a class reader to test students' present reading speed when reading aloud and when reading silently. A class reader will be at a level that will reflect the expected ability of that age group.

    Reading speed can be measured by the students reading aloud for a minute and counting the number of words they read. The process is repeated for silent reading. If the score for reading aloud and reading silently is similar, then the student is reading word for word when reading silently and will be at a disadvantage in the secondary classroom.

    Ask students to time their silent reading speed each day for a week and to keep a daily record to see how much they can improve with effort and practice. It will be easier to use fiction texts initially, the vocabulary will be easier so that poor comprehension of the text will not detract from the overall aim of increasing speed.

2. Model strategies that will increase reading speed.

    - Show students how to scan for key words before reading to get the overall sense of the passage and make comprehension easier. If the student feels they do not understand the information, they will be tempted to slow down and read more carefully or re-read.
    - Demonstrate how to use headings and summaries to focus on the relevant parts of the text and eliminate sections that need not be read.
    - Explain that there is no need to read every word. Students should take in chunks of words, trying to read blocks of three or four words at a time.
    - Explain that it is necessary to keep eyes moving from left to right steadily across the page and to avoid going back over text. The brain will become accustomed to filling in any gaps.
    - Demonstrate the use of a ruler as a tracking tool. Keep the ruler below the line being read and move it down the page steadily, so the eyes are forced to keep pace.
    - Experiment with coloured overlays made from A4 coloured file pockets. These coloured sheets will help some students by reducing distracting contrast between page and print. The students could read sections of the text in turns working in small groups and every time a paragraph has been read, the overlays are exchanged and different colour used.
    - When reading for speed, attention and focus are vital: the student must not be distracted by anything else. Warn students their concentration will drop when they are hungry, tired or uncomfortable.
    - It is always worth checking that the light is adequate before starting to read, everyone's eyes tire quickly when they are strained.
    - Any limitations in vocabulary will slow down reading speed. Students should try to familiarise themselves with the meanings of any unknown words prior to reading.
    - It may be worth the students targeting specific subjects, for example, if they find Geography texts hard to read at speed, they should work on Geography vocabulary.

Student advice sheet: reading speed

After moving into secondary school it becomes increasingly useful to be able to read quickly. This is a skill that will develop with practice.

Reading quickly will be harder with some materials than with others because of the complexity of words that are used, novels being easier to read than complex subject texts.

To increase your reading speed, first choose a text that you can read easily with good understanding. Start at the beginning of a chapter and read for a minute, then count the number of words that you have read. This will give you your reading rate per minute. Record this score and use it as your baseline.

> Read another passage for a minute from the same book the following evening and record your reading rate again. Concentrate on reading as quickly as you can, but still absorbing the meaning of the text. If you do this every evening for two weeks, you will find that your reading speed will gradually increase.
>
> - Try to take in three or four words at a time rather than read word for word.
> - Do not allow yourself to backtrack to check on words, but keep your eyes moving forwards. Your brain will learn to fill in the gaps.
> - Put a ruler or index card under the line that you are reading and move it at a steady pace down the page to maintain speed.
> - Some people find that a coloured transparent A4 sheet placed over the text reduces paper/print contrast and makes reading more comfortable. Old A4 coloured file pockets can be cut in half and used for this.
> - If you get headaches when reading at length, it will be worth having your eyes checked by an optician.
> - When you feel more confident, begin to practise on more complex texts, but remember, reading is all about *comprehension* and not speed.

Lesson 5: Reading comprehension

It is possible for students of all abilities to improve their understanding of reading material. Competent readers automatically use strategies to monitor their comprehension as they read, other students will need to be taught directly how to do this.

Lesson 5(a)

Learning objective

Students will be able to approach a variety of reading tasks using techniques to support their comprehension.

Resources required

- Photocopied articles from a magazine or newspaper as appropriate to the age of the students.
- Highlighters or coloured pencils.

Activities

1. **The promotion of a 'reading for understanding' approach.** The teacher reads a photocopied passage from a subject text or newspaper article to the group. As she reads, the teacher talks through what she is doing and why: the students follow using their own photocopy.

   - I read the title or heading to get an idea of the topic and how it will fit into the module being studied.
   - Then I read the first two sentences of the text to get an idea of the content of the passage.
   - As I read, I'll highlight any keywords that relate to this idea in one colour.
   - I read the rest of the passage to find any supporting evidence, which I highlight in another colour.
   - After reading, I summarise the main ideas for myself.
   - Then I jot down the gist of the passage in my own words.

   The students prepare a second summary in the same way with an alternative piece of text. This can be completed individually, in pairs or small groups. Simple or complex text can be used as is appropriate to the individual or group.

2. **SQ3R (Survey, Question, Read, Recall, Review).** This is a method that is used to read in a purposeful way, enabling the student to make sense of information through scaffolding. The teacher once again models the technique, and the students practise the process individually or in pairs.

   - *Survey.* Look at the title and glance through the contents page and chapter headings to make sure that the book contains the required information.
   - *Question.* Why am I reading this? What do I need to find out? Which sections are going to be most useful?
   - *Read.* I target a chapter to read. As I read, I think about key words and look closely at any visual aids: illustrations, graphs and diagrams.
   - *Recall.* After reading, I think about the chapter, jot down any key facts, relate the information to my prior knowledge and work out some practical examples from everyday life.
   - *Review.* I check that the required information has been taken from the book, recorded appropriately and understood.

3. **Change written text into a diagram.** This could be information taken from a class text, magazine or newspaper. The process of thinking about the information and how to convert it into diagrammatic form will ensure students examine the facts closely. Close reviewing will increase understanding of the information and how the different parts fit into the whole. Examples of possible text-to-diagram activities would include: plotting the career progression of a famous historical figure on a timeline with illustrations, the conversion of written information relating to the development of a geographical feature into diagrammatic form or recoding the relationship between characters in a play in a mind map.

Student advice sheet: reading for note taking

- When taking notes from a book, always check the publication date of the book before reading to ensure that information is current.
- Skim read a passage before you start making notes. It might not contain any relevant information.
- Record page numbers when taking notes to make it easier to refer back to the source at a later date. This sort of record keeping is a good habit to develop; completing accurate bibliographies will be essential in further or higher education.
- Use blank postcards as bookmarks and for notes. Jot brief notes down on the card as you read, when the card is full, file it and start a new one. After reading all of the text, use a treasury tag to order your postcards, read them through highlighting any key information and write a summary out on a side of A4.
- When note taking from a borrowed textbook, photocopy any useful pages, and highlight the information on your copy.
- Read the targeted passage and make summary notes in your own words. This will ensure that you have understood what you have read and that your notes are clear enough for revision purposes. If you have copied directly from the book without thinking, you are unlikely to remember information accurately.

Visualisation

One of the many benefits of reading aloud to children is to give them the opportunity to develop visualisation skills, that is, the ability to create mentally an imaginary pictorial sequence of the story. For students who have only experienced story telling on television, visualisation may be an unfamiliar skill, but one that will have many benefits.

Visualisation is also useful to assist with understanding and memory. Many students will naturally visualise a sequence of information when given work that lends itself to that approach: a fictional passage, a parable or a historical event. However, not every student will be able to do this effectively in every situation. Students may need encouragement initially to make their images multi-sensory: hearing the characters speak, smelling the dinner cooking, feeling the wooden bench that they are sitting on. Richly descriptive texts are most effective in initial lessons to give the best opportunity to practise the technique. Younger students may need to draw a sequence of pictures initially before they are able to visualise mentally.

Lesson 5(b)

Learning objective

The students will be able to visualise orally presented information and use the technique as a comprehension and memory tool.

Resources required

A class reader or subject text.

Activities

- Ask the students to visualise their journey to school and draw four or five simple pictures to illustrate the route: their house, the bus at the bus stop, the High Street, the bus outside the school and walking in through the school gates.
- Read a short passage from a class text. This could be the class reader or a non-fiction passage. The students close their eyes and make a video of the passage in their heads. They illustrate their video in simple cartoon form to represent the sequence of events: stages in baking a Victoria sponge, the balcony scene from *Romeo and Juliet* or the process of longshore drift.
- Read a longer passage or a passage with more detail. Ask the students to work in pairs and describe to their partner how they imagined the characters, objects or environment. Give the pupils lists of specific questions to focus their attention on the detail. What is the main character wearing? Why do they think this? Were there any clues in the story to help or did they use their imagination? What sort of prior knowledge did they use, for example, if the description were of a boy in the 1940s, would he be wearing trainers and a baseball cap? What season did they imagine the action to take place and why did they think this? What did the boy's friends look like? As the students become more experienced in the use of the technique, the text and the questioning can become more complex and detailed.

Lesson 6: Subject-specific vocabulary

It is vital for students to have an understanding of subject-specific words in order to comprehend subject texts. Teaching staff can overestimate students' knowledge of vocabulary and assume understanding where none exists.

Many subject-specific words have everyday equivalents that will confuse some students: conductor, force, contract, positive, charge, cell, bulb and material. A few unfamiliar words within a text may affect a student's understanding.

Most subject departments will have systems that give students access to subject vocabulary lists. These might include:

- Subject-specific vocabulary and definitions accessed through departmental web pages.
- Lists of words specific to a module distributed for discussion during the first lesson on that topic.

- Vocabulary lists given to students at the beginning of each school year.
- Display boards with, for example, items of equipment displayed in graphic form annotated with the correct keywords and definitions.

However, having accessible vocabulary lists does not guarantee that students will use them. Regular, but brief revision sessions during lessons will familiarise all of the students with the words, their pronunciation and correct definitions. Such ten-minute, 'Quick Quiz' sessions can be used as a break within a lesson or for plenary input.

Lesson 6

Learning objective

Students will be able to use and define subject-specific vocabulary with confidence and accuracy.

Resources required

- Class textbooks.
- Post-it notes.
- Pre-prepared DARTS procedures.
- A whiteboard or OHP.
- Small blank cards for use in games.

Activities

Discuss with the students why possessing a good recall of subject words and meanings is essential if they are to progress successfully.

The teacher selects from the following activities as appropriate for student age and ability level:

- Use the word lists from the back of class textbooks. The students work in pairs. One student reads out a word and the other defines it in their own words clearly enough to satisfy their partner.
- 'What am I?'/'Twenty Questions'. Students volunteer to ask the class/group/a partner questions in order to work out who or what a chosen word phrase is. Those students look away while a subject word is written on the whiteboard, for example: rhombus, Lysander, monitor, Gaza Strip, longshore drift, photosynthesis, government, Mediterranean, coastal erosion, Queen Victoria or an equilateral triangle. The word is then erased. The student is allowed to ask 20 questions to try to work out who or what they are.
- Use DARTs (Directed Activity Related to Text) activities. These activities would include: cloze procedures, completion of partially drawn tables, cutting and pasting definitions to the correct word, annotating part of a diagram or converting information into a visual display.
- Word webs and mnemonics can help draw students' attention to word meanings as well as the correct spelling of subject vocabulary. For example, in equal, equilibrium, equation and equilateral, the root word is equa/equi from the Latin, 'to make even'. Homework activities could involve devising and illustrating a mnemonic to help remember word meanings.
- 'Odd Man Out'. The teacher lists groups of words on the OHP or whiteboard. The students work out which word is the odd one out and why or find as many 'odd ones out' as they can: football, squash, badminton, tennis, netball and hockey. The answer could be badminton because it is the only game played with a shuttlecock or netball because it is usually only played by women and girls.
- 'Daisy chains'. Write subject keywords on individual cards in topic sets. The pupils work in pairs to link the words through their meanings into as long a chain as possible. If several sets

of cards are made (respiration, the skeleton, healthy eating, eye sight), use different coloured cards to make it easy to keep the sets separate.
- Draw the students' attention to keyword displays by having a 'Quick Quiz' on the words and their definitions for 5 minutes at the beginning or end of a lesson.
- The equivalent of the board games *Taboo* or *Articulate!* can be played where a specific word has to be described without using the word itself. The member of staff taking the lesson could choose the words from those the students have problems remembering or use the index from a class text, writing the word down for the student selected as 'describer'.
- Play 'Word Loops'. Each student in the class is given a few cards with a subject word on one side of the card and the definition of another word on the other side. One student starts by reading out the definition of a word that is on their card; the student with the corresponding word reads it out and then gives the definition that is on the other half of their card and so on. If the loop is run through a few times and timed, students will be motivated to respond as quickly as possible. The sets of cards could be redistributed to different groups/pairs at the end of each game. If the students make their own cards, they will have extra opportunities to familiarise themselves with the words.
- 1, 2, 3 and Out. The class stand up and the teacher asks students to define a subject word. Incorrect answers lose lives. As the aim is to help the students learn the vocabulary rather than catch them out, the teacher should ask the questions according to the student's individual ability.
- Bingo. The students work in small groups; they each chose six words from the vocabulary list for that module. One of the students reads out definitions for the words from the list in a random order and the other students cross off the corresponding word if it is on their list. The first student with all of their words crossed off wins the game.
- 'Hangman' or 'Blockbusters' played in pairs, groups or as a whole class activity. A student or the teacher can lead the game.
- Card games such as Pelmanism to play in pairs or small groups. If the students are involved in designing the cards or game, they will have discussed the words and their definitions before playing. This gives an additional opportunity for over learning.
- I went to market and bought .... A collection of objects or pictures of objects could be displayed on the OHP and removed when they are correctly named and a definition of their use given.
- Whole class activity. Many subject-specific words have everyday equivalents. Ask students to think of two or three alternative meanings for keywords such as: conductor, force, contact, positive, pitch, charge, cell, pupil, pole, current, bulb, material.
- Some publishers produce a wide selection of photocopiable keyword resources that can be useful for homework tasks or student assessment (see Peppermint Publications: sales@peppermintpublications.co.uk).
- Have a quiz on the meanings of exam or essay instructional vocabulary, as follows:
    1. *Apply* = Explain how an idea or concept would work through the use of examples.
    2. *Assess* = Appraise.
    3. *Compare* = Show similarities and differences between two or more things.
    4. *Contrast* = Highlight the differences between two or more things.
    5. *Discuss* = Provide a detailed description including arguments for and against.
    6. *Explain* = Clarify. Tell why something happened.
    7. *Interpret* = Show the meaning of.
    8. *Justify* = Account for. Give arguments to support your statement.
    9. *Outline* = Condense a topic under main headings with subheadings used as support.
    10. *Relate* = Show connections between ideas and concepts.
    11. *State* = Offer main points without discussion.
    12. *Summarise* = Bring knowledge together with emphasis on the main points.

Part II

Practical exercises, advice sheets and hand-outs to support staff, parents, carers and students

Chapter 6

Advice Sheets

In this chapter you will find the following:

- Advice Sheet 1: Advice for parents – hearing your child read
- Advice Sheet 2: Advice for parents – reading with your child
- Advice Sheet 3: Advice for parents – suggestions for suitable reading resources
- Advice Sheet 4: Assessment of vocabulary and general knowledge
- Advice Sheet 5: Developing active reading – advice for mainstream teachers
- Advice Sheet 6: Games and activities to support the development of subject vocabulary
- Advice Sheet 7: Generic reading comprehension exercises for PHSE and study skills lessons
- Advice Sheet 8: Promoting reading in the form room
- Advice Sheet 9: Resources to support students' reading in withdrawal lessons
- Advice Sheet 10: Slow reading: why it happens and how to help individual readers
- Advice Sheet 11: Student advice sheet – how to improve your comprehension
- Advice Sheet 12: Using newspapers as a reading resource

Advice Sheet 1

Advice for parents – hearing your child read

When children read aloud to adults they need to succeed. They should feel that they are reading for the enjoyment of content, rather than to demonstrate their decoding skills.

Talk about the book before they start to read

- This looks interesting. What do you think it's going to be about? I quite like books about: France/music/gardening/films/golf. Do you like that sort of book? Do you like stories about life in the olden days/in boarding schools/football?

Support reading for meaning

- When they come across any unfamiliar words, try to help them guess their meanings. Ask questions to help them: 'Have a go'; 'What might make sense there?'; 'Can you think what it might be?'
- Encourage the child to use their phonic knowledge: 'What sound does the word begin/end with?'; What do you think the beginning of the word will sound like?
- Encourage them to focus on word parts: 'Can you see any smaller words inside the word?' (wind/mill, stop/watch, dish/wash/er, car/pen/ter); 'That word looks a bit like the word brought or fought, I think it might be nought.'
- Suggest missing the unknown word out and reading on: 'Let's see if we can work it out at the end of this next bit.'
- Read the sentence to show how to use context: 'I'll read it from the beginning and see if we can work out what it might be.' Read the sentence with exaggerated expression.
- Point out any pictorial clues: 'What is the girl jumping over in the picture?'

Responding

- Praise them when they work out a word correctly. If they say 'Is it ....?', and the word is correct, say, 'Let's see if that would make sense. Yes, well done, you got it!' or, 'Does that sound right? Yes, well done, that was tricky.'
- If they are wrong, acknowledge their effort and make light of the error: 'That would be a good word and it would make sense, but the word the writer used in this sentence is ....'
- If a child still can't attempt a word after prompting, read it yourself and move on without comment.
- It is very important to respond to content. If there's a joke, laugh; if there is new information, discuss it, preferably giving the child the chance to share their own knowledge. Express an interest in what's going to happen next.

© 2015, *Transforming Reading Skills in the Secondary School*, Pat Guy, Routledge

When finishing reading

- Always end reading on a positive note: 'I liked that book. The bit about ..... was interesting. I didn't know that until now'; 'I liked the joke about ..... I'll have to try to remember that one to tell Uncle David.'

Advice Sheet 2
Advice for parents – reading with your child

- Read to your child. They can ask you questions about the book that you will be able to answer immediately and at a level appropriate to their needs. Most children enjoy adult attention so a link with individual attention and reading will be a positive one.
- Involve your child in everyday reading. Newspapers, magazines, letters, catalogues, match programmes, school textbooks, web pages, instruction manuals or recipe books are all excellent examples of everyday reading material and will demonstrate how useful reading is in adult life.
- The more factual books your child reads, the better their general knowledge will become. General knowledge is an essential part of good comprehension.
- Point out unusual words as you read and explain their meaning: 'Fan belt, that's the belt that keeps a fan moving inside the engine to cool the motor. The temperature gauge is on the dashboard and lets you know when the engine is getting hot.'
- Point out diagrams or pictures in books to help your child to realise that they will help their understanding.
- Use pictures in books to extend the children's vocabulary: 'There's the fan belt in that diagram'; 'Do you know what we call that part of the bike?'; 'Do you know another word for gigantic?'
- Provide other words that mean the same: 'It says that the storm was horrendous, that means it was absolutely awful.'
- Encourage your child's personal response to stories. Ask 'Do you think it was a good idea to do that? What would you have done if that had happened to you?'
- When reading to your child, stop periodically and talk about what has happened so far. Ask the child to tell you what they think will happen next and then read on to find out if they are right.
- Join the Library yourself and help your child to get a library card.
- Use books as a way in to difficult conversations: a trip to the hospital, the death of a pet, divorce, or as a link across the generations: 'That makes me laugh. It is just the sort of thing that Grandad would have done to tease me when I was your age.'
- When reading to your child, try to read with expression to convey meaning as well as to hold their interest. If necessary, interpret the content: 'I don't think the author really means that's good. He's probably being sarcastic.' Explain the difference between sentences when one is being used sarcastically. 'What a lovely day' will be said differently when the day is sunny and when it is raining heavily.
- Give your children books, comics and magazines as presents or treats.
- Borrow books from the Library about places you may visit on holiday or for days out.
- Set an example as a reader and let your child see you reading.
- Talk to your child about the different parts of a book: front cover, title, index and glossary.
- Take CDs to listen to on car journeys, when visiting relatives or going on holiday.
- Encourage and respond to children's interests by helping them pick out books on their favourite topics: pets, films, music, fashion, *Star Wars*, celebrities, sports or interesting places.
- Show an interest in the stories and books the children select. Ask which their favourites are. If they enjoy books by the same author. Whether they have read others in the same series.

© 2015, *Transforming Reading Skills in the Secondary School*, Pat Guy, Routledge

Advice Sheet 3

Advice for parents – suggestions for suitable reading resources

- Abridged versions of classics can be useful to provide an overview of the original texts being read by the children in school: Shakespeare, Austen, Charlotte and Emily Brontë or Dickens.
- Science fiction and Fantasy adventures from series such as: *A Song of Ice and Fire*, the *Minecraft* series, *The Warrior Chronicles* or *The Sorcery Code*.
- Traditional stories that have stood the test of time are certain to hold some appeal: *The Iron Man, Black Beauty, Treasure Island, The Wind in the Willows, Five Children and It, The Railway Children, The Silver Sword, Tom's Midnight Garden*.
- Focus on the children's favourite authors: Roald Dahl, James Patterson, George R.R. Martin, Anne Fine, Jacqueline Wilson, Enid Blyton or Kate Atkinson, and suggest reading more of their work.
- Books that link to TV series or films can be popular: *Top Gear, Dr Who, The Hunger Games, Dragon's Den*, Jamie Oliver cookbooks or *The Fault in our Stars*.
- Non-fiction books around the children's areas of interest: martial arts, golf, nursing, cookery, music, craft and art, Arsenal FC, rap, caring for a pet, stock cars, art and design, computers, fashion.
- Biographies and autobiographies: political, musical, TV and sports personalities or famous people from History, such as Nelson Mandela, Amy Winehouse, Anne Frank, Mother Teresa, David Beckham, Winston Churchill, the Romans or Queen Victoria.
- Animal books, perhaps fiction such as the *Animal Ark* series, information books about unusual animals (sharks, dinosaurs, reptiles), books about careers with animals or caring for pets.
- After reading one book from, for example, the *Horrible History* Geography and Science series, pupils may be motivated to read more from the sets.
- Books that provide the opportunity to read around school topics will all provide a human perspective to the period, for example: *Carrie's War, Goodnight Mr Tom, The Machine Gunners, The Silver Sword* or *I am David* for the Second World War.
- Newspapers, comics and magazines: *Marvel* comics, *Match, NME, Aquila*, the junior sections of newspapers or *Kerrang*.
- Encyclopaedias, atlases, brochures, instruction manuals, the internet or books from the *I-Spy* series.
- Collections of poetry and verse.
- Comic strip books: Manga, Japanese comics and graphic novels. There are graphic adaptations for most classic works of English Literature that students will be studying in school.
- Puzzle and quiz books: The 'Where's Wally' series, The Usborne series of puzzle adventures and general knowledge quiz books.
- Short stories, perhaps the series written by Paul Jennings or Roald Dahl, or the short stories of Sherlock Holmes.
- Joke, riddle and quiz books.

© 2015, *Transforming Reading Skills in the Secondary School*, Pat Guy, Routledge

Advice Sheet 4

Assessment of vocabulary and general knowledge

- What is another word for the low ground between two hills? (Valley)
- Who was Neil Armstrong? (The first person to walk on the moon)
- What is a song for two called? (Duet)
- What name is given to young kangaroos? (Joey)
- Who was Edward Jenner? (Jenner was the first doctor to vaccinate people against smallpox)
- What is another word for an enclosure for containing birds? (Aviary)
- What is the common name for the spine? (Backbone)
- Who ran the first mile in under four minutes? (Roger Bannister)
- Give an example of an idiom? (Idioms are phrases or expressions that cannot be taken literally, for example, 'It is raining cats and dogs')
- What do we call a field where fruit trees are grown? (Orchard)
- Who wrote *A Christmas Carol*? (Charles Dickens)
- What do we call the meat of a deer? (Venison)
- What is another word for the steps on a ladder? (Rungs)
- Who is credited with the invention of television? (John Logie Baird)
- What is another word for a fertile place in the dessert? (Oasis)
- Who was Rodin? (A French sculptor. An example of his more famous work is *The Thinker*)
- Who was Horatio Nelson? (British naval officer killed in the Battle of Trafalgar, 1805)
- What does the acronym RSVP mean? (Répondez s'il vous plaît)
- Who was Margaret Thatcher? (The first female British Prime Minister)
- What is another word for a substance used to counteract poisoning, for example, in a snake bite? (Antidote)
- What is another name for a place where fish are kept? (Aquarium)
- Who was Long John Silver? (A pirate in the book *Treasure Island*)
- What is another word for shallow crossing in a river? (Ford)
- What is another word for the shiny material often used to make wedding dresses? (Satin/silk)

© 2015, *Transforming Reading Skills in the Secondary School*, Pat Guy, Routledge

Advice Sheet 5

Developing active reading – advice for mainstream teachers

- Activate the students' existing background knowledge of the subject or topic by listening to an extract from literature related to the topic, watching a video or YouTube clip or holding a class/group discussion.
- Add new material to information that is already familiar, perhaps by reading from a previous Key Stage text. This will set the scene and make links between new information and prior knowledge.
- Use 'reading theatre techniques' to read material in class. Divide the text into short sections and distribute the sections among students to be read aloud in groups or chorally. The teacher could take the main headlines, bullet points could be read chorally and supporting evidence read in pairs. The material could be read several times with the need for expression and emphasis stressed to make facts as clear as possible. This technique is fun and will ensure more student engagement than when a 'reading around the class' approach is taken.
- Consider the sort of reading students will need to do in the specific subject: analysis, research, skimming, scanning or close reading. These processes may need to be taught directly.
- Ensure students are clear about the purpose of any reading. If students know what approaches they should take before they read, they will be more focused on what is required from the activity. This could be done initially as a teacher modelling activity: 'We need to find out about the electro-magnetic spectrum, so we'll start by looking at the contents page and index in the book. We may need to look up unfamiliar terms in the glossary and examine illustrations and diagrams to help our understanding. We could explain the ideas in our own words, look up the summary to see if we are correct or check our understanding with another student. If we are still confused, we could look at another source of information to see if that makes the facts we need any clearer.'
- Teach any unfamiliar technical expressions and vocabulary before giving reading tasks. Abstract words may prove harder to define; it would be worth taking the time to increase students' understanding of these before reading. Be aware of specialist meanings of words. For example, the sum, 'Find the product of 60 and 32' is easy in itself, but the meaning of the word 'product' may cause uncertainty.
- When students experience confusions over word meanings, they will create their own interpretations. These may appear nonsensical to others and so add to their difficulties. It is always worth spending some time checking students' understanding of subject vocabulary. They may not realise that words can have several different meanings. Here are some examples:
    - *Current*: Water that has a continuous movement, a flow of electric charge or something that is happening at the moment?
    - *Conductor*: Is this someone who collects fares and checks tickets, a person who conducts an orchestra or a substance that conducts electricity?
    - *Plane*: A mathematical shape, an aeroplane or a carpenter's tool for smoothing wood?
    - *Pitch*: A playing field, the alternate dip and rise of the bow and stern of a ship, the angle of a roof or the relative position of a tone within a range of musical sounds?
    - *Force*: Is this an influence producing a change or to make someone do something they don't want to do

© 2015, *Transforming Reading Skills in the Secondary School*, Pat Guy, Routledge

Advice Sheet 6

Games and activities to support the development of subject vocabulary

These activities could be used as warm-ups at the beginning of lessons to remind students of the content matter of the current topic or during plenary sessions to consolidate learning.

Activity 1

Match the word with the correct definition from jumbled sets of vocabulary:

- *Simile* = Comparisons which don't use 'like' or 'as', but say that something 'is' something else because it is similar, for example, 'Life is a journey'.
- *Hyperbole* = A word that imitates the sound it represents, for example, 'Pop'.
- *Onomatopoeia* = Figurative language that exaggerates, for example, 'I nearly died laughing'.
- *Alliteration* = Giving inanimate objects human characteristics, for example, 'The wind howled'.
- *Personification* = Repetition of a consonant in a phrase, for example, 'Sizzling sausages in the saucepan'.

Activity 2

Find the English/Geographical/Home Economics/German vocabulary word searches and crosswords.

Activity 3

This activity is known as 'Subject Ten Questions'. Information about an object, person, event or material gradually becomes more specific with each clue. The students have ten attempts to guess the word, losing a point with each incorrect guess. For example:

1. This is a city.
2. The city is in Europe.
3. It is sometimes known as the 'City of Dreams'.
4. It is home to the world's oldest zoo.
5. This city is famous for coffee houses.
6. It is famous for Sachertorte.
7. The Danube runs through the city centre.
8. Schubert and Strauss were born here.
9. The city is the capital of Austria.
10. The name of the city starts with a 'V'.

© 2015, *Transforming Reading Skills in the Secondary School*, Pat Guy, Routledge

Activity 4

Encourage students to increase their speedy recognition of subject vocabulary by reading aloud from the glossaries at the back of class textbooks. They chose one page of words and definitions to read quietly to themselves, recording the time taken. When reading the page on subsequent occasions, they try to improve their time. Repeat the activity at the end of five consecutive lessons. Suggest to the students that they start on the first day at a steady reading rate to ensure improvement. Starting slowly will necessitate more careful reading, guaranteeing maximum focus on the task.

Activity 5

Create an interactive word bank on a classroom wall. Use colour and different print fonts to make the words visually memorable. Teachers could target five or six keywords from the current topic for focus during the week, gradually building a word bank for interactive games based around subject keyword recognition and accurate definition.

Activity 6

Many subject-specific words have everyday equivalents that confuse students. The scientific words: conductor, force, contact, positive, charge, cell, pupil, bulb and material all have everyday alternatives. Just a few puzzling words within a text can restrict a student's understanding of written text. To demonstrate words that have several meanings, ask the students to make subject-specific vocabulary lists for their own hobbies and interests. This will show the importance of being aware of alternative meanings of words and registering context to ensure what is read makes sense. Here are some examples from netball:

- *Shot*: He shot his rifle. She shot the winning goal.
- *Centre*: The hole was in the centre of the scarf. She played Centre in the match.
- *Third*: I live in the third house on the street. The player was in the goal third.
- *Pass*: Did he pass his driving test? The Centre's first pass went wide.
- *Post*: Colin's Granddad will post the card today. The post blew over in the middle of the match.
- *Wing*: The bird has a broken wing. Sadie will play on the wing for this game.
- *Court*: Henry VII held court at the castle. Our netball court is behind the Science lab.

Activity 7

'Who/What/Where am I?' A student volunteers to come up to the front of the class and face the other students with their back to the board. The teacher writes a subject-specific word on the board. The student is allowed to ask the other students a set number of questions to try to work out who, where or what the word is. The number of questions and their level of difficulty are dependent on the students' age and ability level. Suitable vocabulary might include: a rhombus, river delta, Lysander, Gaza, a keyboard, photosynthesis, the Conservative Party, the Mediterranean, Queen Victoria or an equilateral triangle. Allow students to choose the word to write on the board; a competitive nature will ensure they select what they believe to be the most difficult words to test their peers. The teacher can note those words which seem to give most problems and record these words for future reference.

© 2015, *Transforming Reading Skills in the Secondary School*, Pat Guy, Routledge

Activity 8

The equivalent of the board game *Articulate!* can be played where a subject-specific word has to be described without using the actual word. The member of staff taking the lesson could choose subject-specific vocabulary from the index of a class textbook, writing the word down for the student selected as 'describer'. Selecting vocabulary from the index of the class textbook will reinforce the use of different parts of a book for reference.

Activity 9

Play 'Word Loops' (Word and definition dominoes). Students are divided into groups and given two sheets of blank A4 paper. They fold each piece of paper to create 16 rectangles. They then cut or tear the 32 rectangles out. The students write a subject word on one rectangle with the definition of that word on the back of another rectangle. They then turn over the piece of paper with the definition on and write another word on the reverse and then write the definition of that word on the next rectangle and so on until all the pieces of paper have been used and a loop of words and definitions created. The cards are shuffled and shared amongst the group. One student in the group reads out the definition on their card; the student with the matching word reads it out and gives the definition that is on the reverse of their paper and so on. If the loop is read through a few times and timed, students will be motivated to recognise and pronounce their word and give the new definition as quickly as possible. The cards can be redistributed to different groups after every few games. The fact that the cards are made from paper and therefore not durable does not matter; learning will occur whilst the cards are being made and so the quality of the end product is unimportant.

Activity 10

List as many subject-specific words relating to, for example, the coast, volcanoes, circles, English grammar, magnetism, the skeleton, emancipation or electricity as you can in two minutes. Work in pairs or small groups to introduce a competitive element.

Activity 11

Play the game 'Ten'. Students design ten keywords quizzes for different letters of the alphabet as a test for their peers. The clue must be a definition:

- *Legend*: A small table accompanying the map that explains the symbols used.
- *Longitude*: The angular distance east or west from the north–south line that passes through Greenwich.
- *Lake*: A large body of water surrounded by land on all sides.
- *Latitude*: The angular distance north or south from the equator to a location.

Activity 12

Maths vocabulary sheets could be used for reference, definition and or spelling tests/games.

MATHS 1	SET ONE			
WORD	DEFINITION			
1. Acute angle	An angle of less than 90 degrees			

© 2015, *Transforming Reading Skills in the Secondary School*, Pat Guy, Routledge

2. Anticlockwise	To move in the opposite way to the hands of a clock			
3. Arc	Part of the circumference of a circle			
4. Area	The space inside a plane figure			
5. Circumference	All the way round a circle			
6. Clockwise	To move in the same direction as the hands of a clock			
7. Cube	A solid shape with six square faces			
8. Cuboid	A solid shape with six rectangular faces			
9. Decrease	To make smaller			
10. Diameter	The distance across the middle of a circle			

MATHS 1	**SET TWO**			
Word	**Definition**			
1. Digit	A single figure			
2. Estimate	The rough answer			
3. Factor	A number that divides into another number			
4. Hexagon	A plane figure with six sides			
5. Horizontal	Straight across. Parallel to the horizon			
6. Increase	To make something larger			
7. Locus	The path of a moving object			
8. Mean	Average			
9. Median	The middle of a set of numbers placed in order of size			
10. Mode	The number that occurs most often in a set of numbers			

MATHS 1	**SET THREE**			
Word	**Definition**			
1. Negative	Less than nought			
2. Obtuse angle	An angle that is less than 180 degrees, but more than 90 degrees			
3. Octagon	A plane figure with eight sides			
4. Parallel	Lines which are always the same distance apart			
5. Pentagon	A plane figure with five sides			
6. Per cent	Out of a hundred			
7. Perimeter	The complete distance around the outside of a figure			
8. Plane figure	A flat figure			
9. Polygon	A plane figure with many sides			
10. Prime number	A number which has only two factors, itself and one			

© 2015, *Transforming Reading Skills in the Secondary School*, Pat Guy, Routledge

Specialist vocabulary for exams can pose a problem for some students. It is important to be able to understand the meanings of instruction words used in exam questions and to respond appropriately: an 'explanation' of a situation requiring a different response to an 'analysis' of a situation. The students' attention will need to be drawn to these instruction words to ensure they are aware of subtle differences in meaning and are given adequate practice in matching words and definitions. Answering exam questions from old papers will be essential for pupils with poor language skills: they may know the information, but not understand what the question requires by way of a response. Bullet point answers to exam questions will help students to become more aware of the appropriateness of their responses without having to waste time writing out complete essays.

Here is a list of command words used in exam questions and their definitions:

- *Analyse*: Take apart a concept or a process, and explain it step by step.
- *Compare*: Show likenesses and differences when comparing two events, theories, or processes.
- *Contrast*: Show differences between two processes or theories.
- *Define*: Provide a definition of a key term.
- *Demonstrate*: Provide proof of your answer by using an example.
- *Discuss*: Demonstrate that you know the strengths and weaknesses of both sides of an argument.
- *Explain*: Provide an answer that gives a 'why' response. Give an overview of the problem and a solution for a particular issue.
- *Illustrate*: Use examples to show or explain a topic.
- *Justify*: Use examples or evidence to show why (in your opinion) information is correct.
- *Order*: Provide a chronological or value-based answer by listing several items, terms or events in correct placement.
- *Relate*: Show a relationship between two events or items by discussing their similarities.
- *Prove*: Use evidence (this could be numbers) or reasoning to solve a problem.

© 2015, *Transforming Reading Skills in the Secondary School*, Pat Guy, Routledge

Advice Sheet 7

Generic reading comprehension exercises for PHSE and study skills lessons

- Pick out ten of the verbs, nouns or adjectives in a passage and replace them with words that have the same meaning.
- Rewrite a chapter from a different character's point of view: the mother's, her child's, a neighbours' or the family pet's. Track all the action that involves that individual.
- Read a passage and think of ten comprehension questions relating to the passage for a partner to answer. The questions could include inference that might be answered later in the text, so your partner has to make informed guesses.
- Read a story in a small group of three or four students. Then each of the students is given a number. Student number one starts to retell the story, after 15 seconds student number two takes over and then student three and student four until the whole story is retold.
- Pick out one topic sentence that summarises the text.
- Pick out six words to give the key information of the text.
- Identify the main ideas and supporting detail of a text and show their relationship in a mind map.
- Design a poster to recommend the text to other readers explaining what they will gain from reading this book.
- Make a graphic display from the information in the text: draw a timeline for the sequence of events, a mind map of characters and their relationships, a cause and effect grid, or a concept map to represent all the information contained in each chapter.
- Summarise a passage in a certain number of sentences. Students may need help initially to tackle summaries in a logical way, perhaps working on a text as a class, highlighting any keywords or ideas, crossing out padding and rephrasing the main ideas.
- Paraphrase textbook language into colloquial English, for example, changing the formal, antiquated language used in classic texts into modern day English.
- List all the facts, opinions or emotions that can be found in a passage.
- Ask questions using the six question words: who, why, when, what, where, and how.
- List everything the reader could find out about a text by examining the title, chapters, blurb and illustrations.

© 2015, *Transforming Reading Skills in the Secondary School*, Pat Guy, Routledge

Advice Sheet 8
Promoting reading in the form room

- Have a bulletin board in the form room promoting books and other reading material relating to specific subjects: history books, science magazines, favourite French authors or geographical information relating to school trips.
- Arrange a 'New to Me' book introduction each week when a teacher or student gives a brief review, presents an oral report or a poster about a book they have enjoyed recently. Hold a contest with competing books for 'New Book of the Month'.
- Appoint a student to be 'Reader for the Day'. It will be their responsibility to read all class announcements and any registration messages.
- Hold Book Fairs across year groups where students can exchange magazines, comics and books with other classes.
- Read aloud regularly to the class: a whole book, interesting parts from a book, the first chapter or extracts about a specific character. Some readers may be motivated to read the whole book.
- Read poetry and help the class learn poems by heart.
- Hold individual reading conferences with students. Discuss the books they are reading and suggest similar books they might enjoy.
- Keep a 'Books I have read' chart. Encourage individual progress and competition between classes.
- Tie in books to other subjects: 'I wonder what was happening in America at the time that this book was written.' 'Was the radio invented then?' 'Where else in the world have volcanoes erupted?'

© 2015, *Transforming Reading Skills in the Secondary School*, Pat Guy, Routledge

Advice Sheet 9

Resources to support students' reading in withdrawal lessons

If reading development has proved problematic for students, they are unlikely to choose to read in their spare time. They may avoid reading in class because of a lack of fluency and so a vicious circle is established. Without practice, reading will remain slow and hesitant. If a student is asked to read aloud in a mainstream lesson, they will be concerned about appearing competent in front of their peers and so all of their effort will be focused on decoding (reading the words), with little attention paid to meaning. When students read during support lessons, individually or in pairs or small groups, they will be less concerned about making errors. This sort of regular reading practice will improve both their confidence and fluency. The more automatic their decoding, the more attention the student can give to understanding. When a student reads aloud, the teacher will be able to monitor their skills discretely and target support strategies as appropriate for that individual.

Resources

- Plays are a popular reading resource with older students. Spirals Plays published by Nelson Thornes are one example of a good series of comedy plays. The texts comprise a few parts, with short pieces of dialogue to be read by each character. The scenes are brief allowing parts to be changed regularly. If the students are allowed to act out the plays, they will be given a legitimate opportunity to move around the room. Such fun activities in withdrawal lessons can improve student confidence and they may begin to volunteer for small parts in plays read within the mainstream class.

> Some material that is designed to motivate reluctant readers can appear patronising and based on stereotypical assumptions. All students need well-written, interesting texts whatever their level of skill.

- EAL readers are of value as abridged versions of classics. The simplified vocabulary makes the texts easier for the students to decode. Often the only problem for the reader will be deciphering the characters' names (Anatole Garron, Raoul D'Aubert, Bronia Balicki), so agree within the group to change difficult names to easily remembered ones for purposes of fluency. Ant for Anatole, Rich for Raoul and Betty for Bronia. Abridged texts cannot replace original material, but will give students a good overview of the plot and characters and the student will be happy to be reading 'age appropriate' texts, albeit in a reduced form. Established publishers such as Oxford University Press produce a huge range of popular modern readers: *Moby Dick*, *A Christmas Carol*, *Emma*, *The Secret Garden*, *Jane Eyre*, *Wuthering Heights*, *The Hound of the Baskervilles*, *The Strange Case of Dr Jekyll and Mr Hyde*, *Pride and Prejudice*, *Oliver Twist*, *The Elephant Man*, *Ugly Betty*, *Rabbit-Proof Fence*, *The Joy Luck Club* and *The Phantom of the Opera*.

© 2015, *Transforming Reading Skills in the Secondary School*, Pat Guy, Routledge

- Some EAL readers have a CD to accompany the book, enabling the student to follow the text as they listen to the CD. Allow students to draw cartoons of the action as they listen if this helps with concentration.
- Non-fiction may be a student's reading material of choice. Many individuals find fiction long-winded, and prefer non-fiction for its snappier approach. When they need to find information relating to an interest or hobby, there will be an additional purpose to the activity. A non-fiction piece may be short enough to read in five minutes, yet give a useful boost to the student's general knowledge.
- There are reading programmes available for use with students which can be supervised by adults without specialist training. A good example being 'Toe by Toe', a programme that works on the older student's decoding skills. Such programmes can be used to promote home–school liaison by involving parents in supporting their child at weekends or during holidays (www.toe-by-toe.co.uk).
- Collect magazines and newspaper articles. Tabloid newspapers have a low reading age and run succinct reports and articles on numerous topics that may be of interest to students: fashion, sport, music, hobbies, current affairs, TV and film reviews. Weekend papers tend to run articles summarising the week's events and give useful overviews.
- Collections of short stories can be an alternative for those readers who find the thought of a complete book daunting.
- Have a Joke Day or Riddle Week where students are encouraged to read from joke or riddle books or select a Joke or Riddle of the Day:
    - Q: Why is a river rich? A: Because it has two banks.
    - Q: When is a car not a car? A: When it turns into a drive.
    - Q: What do you get if you cross a cat with a lemon? A: A sour puss.
    - Knock, knock. Who's there? Doris. Doris who? Doris locked, that's why I knocked.

> Jokes and riddles give additional opportunities to explain inference and communicate the fact that words can send several messages.

- 'Listening Books' is an association that enables students to download or stream texts via the internet. A school can purchase a licence for several users for a nominal charge. Listening Books has a wide range of fiction, non-fiction, classics and set texts as well as popular reading material and the association will be a useful first port of call for students who need to read more complex texts in English Literature lessons (www.listening-books.org.uk).
- Charity shops sell DVDs of classic texts at a minimal cost. It can be useful to break a reading session with a short showing of the scene from the book to consolidate student understanding.
- Borrow books, story CDs and DVDs from the local library to use in lessons to give access to a wider selection of material.
- For a change, play card games. A number of board games, for example, *Trivial Pursuit* or trading games require players to read from a set of directions or questions.
- Have flash card competitions where students try to read words or phrases on flash cards as quickly as they can and improve on their previous times.
- Manga is an art form that is appreciated by a lot of students and perfect for eye catching display work. Many Shakespearean classics have been reproduced in a manga format. This material does not replace the original, but can be useful to give the student the gist of the story or play.

© 2015, *Transforming Reading Skills in the Secondary School*, Pat Guy, Routledge

Support

- Share reading amongst the group or between the student and yourself: one paragraph, half a page, one page depending on the students' level of fluency.
- Some students will find it hard to sit still and focus when they are not the one reading, so allow non-readers to be quietly active as they listen. There are lots of cheap, suitable resources: colouring black and white line drawings or mosaic patterns, tracing over magazine pictures, paper cutting activities or handwriting exercises.
- Experiment with ways to make reading more visually comfortable. Coloured overlays cut from plastic A4 folders could be placed over the text to reduce glare. Experiment to see if individuals have preferences between different coloured sheets.
- Use a ruler to track sentences or allow the student to track with their finger. Emphasise at every possible opportunity to the student that they are responsible for their own learning and they must find and use ways to help themselves.
- Read aloud to students and encourage them to visualise the action of the text as they listen. Ask questions to help them to focus their imagination: 'Is it spring or summer?'; 'What is the boy wearing?'; 'Is the sea calm?'. Many students do not visualise when reading, perhaps as a result of watching television: television does not require the viewer to mentally re-create settings and characters in the same way as is necessary when listening to a story.
- Do not be afraid to judge a book too tedious to continue reading after a few chapters. Reading is meant to be a pleasure not a chore and students should feel able to make a judgement about a book and decide whether or not it will be of interest to them.
- Choral reading or group oral reading. Choral reading allows confident readers to lead and the less confident to follow. Poetry can provide interesting material for this sort of activity. Choral reading gives the less confident student the chance to experience fluent reading.
- Enter students for Speech and Drama qualifications. Some students enjoy performing set pieces and qualifications awarded by such associations as LAMDA can provide additional motivation.

Advice Sheet 10

Slow reading: why it happens and how to help individual readers

Try to establish the reason why students might be reading slowly.

Q: *Do you have a problem maintaining concentration?*
A: Try reading at those times when you can concentrate well, perhaps first thing in the morning or mid-afternoon. Avoid reading if you are excessively tired or hungry. Read for a set period of time with regular breaks, particularly when you are not particularly interested in the material. If your mind is constantly wandering have a break and move about before returning to the reading. Try to read in a quiet place with as few distractions as possible. Keep a notepad handy and if you start to think about something else, jot the distracting idea down to think about later, then return to your reading.

Q: *Do you feel that you read slowly out of habit?*
A: Practise reading quickly. Focus on speed and do not allow yourself to go back over the material. Practise initially with easy material and gradually move to more complex texts. Always stay aware of your reading speed.

Q: *Do you read word for word?*
A: Look for keywords and skip over smaller, less important ones. Focus on the overall theme of the text rather than the detail. Practise looking at several words at once, rather than one word at a time.

Q: *Do you attempt to remember every single thing you have read?*
A: Review the material regularly as you read, focusing on understanding the overview. Important points will be repeated and detail is not so relevant. Remind yourself that you need to remember the main issues and not the padding.

Q: *Do you have limited reading experience?*
A: Read every day: any skill will improve with practice.

Q: *Do you feel you have to re-read material?*
A: You may be reading so slowly that by the time you reach the end of the text, you have forgotten what was said at the beginning. Do not worry about the detail, focus on the overview. Important ideas will be mentioned several times and give you the essence of the information.

Q: *Do you have visual difficulties, losing your place easily, experiencing blurring or apparent movement of words?*
A: Make an appointment to see an optometrist and get your eyes checked for any unidentified focusing or tracking problems.

© 2015, *Transforming Reading Skills in the Secondary School*, Pat Guy, Routledge

Q: *Do you process information slowly?*
A: Understanding texts can be a problem when subject material is unfamiliar, but your comprehension will improve as you learn more about the topic. Try reading easier texts (KS2 or KS3 books), on the same subject to help you to clarify ideas. Look up and familiarise yourself with the subject vocabulary used most frequently in that topic.

Q: *Do you think you have eyesight problems?*
A: If you are getting headaches or your eyes feel uncomfortable when you read, go to the optician to have your eyesight checked. If you have been prescribed glasses, make sure you wear them.

© 2015, *Transforming Reading Skills in the Secondary School*, Pat Guy, Routledge

Advice Sheet 11

Student advice sheet – how to improve your comprehension

- Read easier textbooks. Year 7 texts rather than Year 9 or Year 9 texts rather than Year 11. These books will help you to sort out confusions by presenting the same information, but in a simpler way.
- Look closely at any diagrams, charts or graphs in books, they will show how facts link together and present a mass of information in a clear, visual format.
- When reading from a passage, try to summarise facts in your own words. Write out brief notes as if you were texting a friend. Talk aloud to yourself: 'So what this is really saying is that…'. If you cannot summarise information in your own words, you have not understood it properly.
- Enlarge any detailed text on a photocopier and then look at one section at a time.
- Ask your teacher to explain the information in a different way, perhaps using diagrams rather than words or relating the information to practical, everyday examples.
- Ask other students to explain information. They may be able to explain a difficult concept in everyday language. People of your own age may have just grasped concepts themselves and so are more likely to understand your confusions. Teachers, who have been familiar with the information for years, may not realise how complicated some ideas can seem to students who have not come across the concepts before.
- Think about what you already know about the topic and see if you can understand how the new information fits in.
- Pretend that you are teaching someone else the information: a younger pupil, your sister, the lady next door or your Nan.
- Draw a cartoon sequence of the most important events in the passage.
- Skim read a chapter before reading in depth to make sure you have the gist of the content.
- Read difficult passages aloud. Recording a passage on your phone and then playing it back will leave you free to concentrate on meaning.
- Create a mind map of the material, checking that you record all of the key points.
- Highlight and then list all the facts, or all the dates or all the names in a passage.
- Watching videos, television programmes or reading fiction related to the topic, will add to your background knowledge and help you to make sense of what is happening.
- If you are having problems reading *and* understanding a set book, borrow a CD version from the library: then concentrate on understanding the story line as it is read to you.
- Set English Readers are popular as EAL (English as an Additional Language) texts. Libraries and bookshops will stock these series. The readers are simplified versions of the originals and will give you an overview of the plot and characters. Some of the books also have CDs to listen to whilst following the written text in the book.
- Run through recent work in your head before starting to read to refresh your memory and help you tune in to the material as quickly as possible.
- Keep subject-specific dictionaries, your class textbook or a thesaurus to hand to look up the meanings of unfamiliar subject words.
- Test yourself on the meanings of five words from the index of your class textbook each evening. The more subject-specific words you understand, the greater your comprehension will be.

© 2015, *Transforming Reading Skills in the Secondary School*, Pat Guy, Routledge

Advice Sheet 12

Using newspapers as a reading resource

Newspapers offer unlimited opportunity for high interest, purposeful, every day reading.

- Find and record all of the words and pictures that belong to one category: international politics, football, film reviews, horse racing, food, home, animals, business news and fashion.
- Which gender features most in the paper and under what topics?
- Using a local paper, make a list of all the different activities and events scheduled for that weekend.
- Find a news event that happened in another country. Find out ten interesting facts about that country.
- In pairs, make a list of all the different abbreviations you can find in the paper in 15 minutes and define them: HQ, RIP, UN, VIP, CEO and EU.
- Find four news items about government, three articles about people, two articles about business and two about different sports.
- Track the news for a week and identify three problems facing the local area/country/world.
- Make a list of all the countries mentioned in the newspaper during one week. Are the same countries mentioned the following week? Make a data table and bar graph of the results to show where news is happening.
- Classify types of front-page stories for one week and record the results in a visual format. Collect headlines from front pages of different newspapers and discuss the relative importance of stories. Why do certain papers run certain headlines?
- Have a newspaper treasure hunt. Locate one news story, a human interest story, an obituary, editorial, graph or chart, sports report, weather forecast, one advert for clothing and a political cartoon. Record the time taken by each group, pair or individual.

© 2015, *Transforming Reading Skills in the Secondary School*, Pat Guy, Routledge

Glossary

accommodation The way in which the eye focuses on objects at different distances.
antonyms Words with opposite meanings.
automaticity in reading The ability to recognise words automatically and accurately.
Bloom's taxonomy A list of learning objectives relating to reading comprehension levels ranging from easiest to most difficult. When hearing students read, try to include more complex reasoning as well as straightforward recall:

1. *Knowledge.* The reader recalls facts, terms, basic concepts and answers.
2. *Comprehension.* The reader is involved in organising, comparing, translating, interpreting, giving descriptions, and stating the main ideas.
3. *Application.* The reader uses the new knowledge.
4. *Analysis.* The reader makes inferences and finds evidence to support generalisations.
5. *Synthesis.* The reader compiles information from the text in a different way.
6. *Evaluation.* The reader is able to present and defend opinions by making judgements about information.

CVC words Words that are composed of consonant, vowel, consonant, for example: cat, dog, mop, tip, cup, red.
decoding Decoding is the ability to apply your knowledge of letter–sound relationships in order to correctly pronounce written words.
EAL English as an Additional Language.
functionally illiterate When an individual's reading and writing skills are below the level that is required to manage daily living and employment tasks.
genre The kind of language, such as: conversation, a speech, poetry or an advertisement.
grammar The system of rules that govern how words and sentences are constructed.
grapheme Letter or letter combinations ('f' or 'ph') that represent a sound.
homophones Words with different meanings that sound the same: reign/rain, knew/new, bear/bare.
idiom An expression whose meaning cannot be understood from the usual meanings of its constituent parts, for example, 'to kick the bucket' meaning 'to die'.
inference The underlying meaning of material that has to be inferred and is not directly stated.
lexis The vocabulary of a language.
listening comprehension Understanding speech.
modelling Demonstrating processes used by experienced and proficient individuals.
morphemes The smallest meaningful part of a word.
onset and rime Onset is the initial consonant or consonant blend before the vowel, and rime is the vowel and any consonants that follow it: st/ay, m/ay, pl/ay, str/ay, g/ay, w/ay, d/ay, br/ay.
phoneme A phoneme is the smallest part of sound in speech.
phonics An approach to reading that emphasises letter–sound relationship.

phonology The study of sounds in English; how they are produced and how they are combined to make words.

prefix A prefix is an affix which is placed before the stem of a word: post/natal, post/mortem, post/war.

reading fluency To read with accuracy and expression at a rate that focuses on making meaning.

rhyme A word with an ending that sounds similar to the ending of another word: rink, sink, think, drink and shrink.

semantic knowledge Understanding the meaning of words.

synonyms Words that have similar meanings.

syntax Syntax are the grammatical rules of a language by which words are linked together to make sense.

syllables The parts of a word that can be said with interruption: the beats in a word.

synthetic phonics A method of teaching reading which teaches the pupil the letter sounds and then blends these sounds together to read whole words.

word families A group of words that share common rhymes: all, tall, stall, ball, call, and fall.

References and resources

Works cited and further reading

Barton, G. (2013) *Don't Call it Literacy*. Routledge.
Betts, E.A. (1946) *Foundations of Reading Instruction with Emphasis on Differentiated Guidance*. American Book Company.
Cain, K. (2010) *Reading Development and Difficulties*. BPS Blackwell.
Conti-Ramsden, G. and Botting, N. (1999) 'Classification of Children with Specific Language Impairment: Longitudinal Considerations'. *Journal of Speech, Language, and Hearing Research*, 42: 1195–1204.
David, A. (2014) *Help Your Child Love Reading: A Parents' Guide*. Egmont.
Dean, G. (2005) *Teaching Reading in the Secondary Schools*. David Fulton.
Didou, D. (2014) *The Secret of Literacy*. Independent Thinking Press.
Elkin, S. (2010) *Unlocking the Reader in Every Child*. Ransom Publishers.
Gunning, T. (2012) *Reading for All Students*. John Wiley.
Hasbrouck, J. and Tindal, G.A. (2006) *Oral Reading Fluency: 90 Years of Measurement*. The Reading Teacher.
International Reading Association (2000) *Teaching all Children to Read: The Roles of the Reading Specialist*. Pamphlet.
Rasinski, T. and Hamman, P. (2010) 'Fluency: Why It is Not Hot'. *Reading Today*, 28(1): 26.
Ruttle, K. (2009) *You Can Motivate Reluctant Readers*. Scholastic.
Sage, R. (1998) *Communication Support for Students in Senior Schools*. University of Leicester.
Sutton Trust and the Education Endowment Foundation (2012) *The Teaching and Learning Toolkit*.
Tyrer, G. and Taylor, P. (2013) *The Literacy Leaders' Toolkit*. Bloomsbury.

Societies and groups

Booktrust: www.bookstrustchildrensbooks.org.uk
Federation of Children's Book Groups: www.fcbg.org.uk
National Literacy Trust: www.literacytrust.org.uk
ReadingZone.com: www.readingzone.com
Scottish Book Trust: www.scottishbookstrust.com
The Guardian: www.guardian.co.uk/childrens-books-site
The Poetry Trust: www.thepoetry trust.org
The School Librarian: www.sla.org.uk
UK Children's Books: www.ukchildrensbooks.co.uk
UK Literacy Association: www.ukla.org

Index

abridged texts 24, 46, 54, 79, 89
abstract thinking 9
accessibility, school libraries 51
active reading 33; teacher advice sheet 81
advice, libraries as source 51
advice sheets: active reading 81; assessment of vocabulary and general knowledge 80; comprehension 94; encouraging reading 50–1; form room reading 88; hearing children read 76–7; PHSE and study skills 87; reading for note taking 68; reading resources 79; reading speed 66–7; reading with child 78; slow readers 92–3; subject-specific vocabulary 82–6; using newspapers 95; vocabulary development 63; withdrawal lessons 89–91
age of school entry, and reading development 12–13
alternative meanings 71, 83
analysis 39
antonyms 10, 61
Articulate! 71, 84
associations and organisations 49
attention problems 11–12
audio-visual materials 47
auditory discrimination 7
auditory memory 15–16
authors' visits 48
autobiographies 23

barriers to reading development: attention problems 11–12; auditory memory 15–16; developmental delay 12–13; general knowledge 11; hearing loss 4–5; language skills 6–7; learning styles 13–14; overview 4; restricted vocabulary 7–10; teaching methods 13–14; undiagnosed medical problems 4–6; visual memory 14–15; visual problems 5–6
Betts, E.A. 30
Bingo 71
biographies 23
Blockbusters 71
book: glossary 96–7; overview 3
book clubs 48, 51
book competitions, shadowing 49, 51
book lists 53
book recommendations 48
book reviews 54
book sales 49
book series, for reading practice 23
Botting, N. 6
bottom-up teaching 13

'Call my Bluff' 60
card games 71
cartoons 63
CDs 52, 90
character names 41
chattiness, masking problems 9
choice, and motivation 46
choral activities 16, 22, 30, 38, 40, 91
cinema trips 49
classroom displays 40
cliff hangers 27
close reading 33, 57
cloze exercises 39
clues, and vocabulary development 10
college level readers, types 17–18
colour, use of 44
coloured overlays 5, 6, 44, 66, 91
comics 23, 24, 47
communicating, information from texts 37
competitions 51
complexity, and reading speed 43
comprehension: and decoding 33–4; examination instructions 41; extending vocabulary 40–1; fiction 34; lessons for 67–9; non-fiction 35–9; parents/carers advice sheet 76; PHSE and study skills 87; practice 36; and reading speed 43; student advice sheet 94; use of diagrams 38; use of drama 38; visualisation 38–9, 68–9
comprehension development 26–8, 33–41
comprehension levels 18; checking 27; reader questions 19
concentration, and reading speed 43, 44
Conti-Ramsden, G. 6
crosswords 82
curiosity, and vocabulary development 10

DARTs (Directed Activities Related to Text) 39, 70
decoding: and comprehension 33–4; errors 18; problems 6–7; reader questions 19
developmental delay 12–13
diagrams, use of 38, 68
diaries 62
dictionaries: games with 61, 62–3; for reading practice 23; use of 10, 54
discussion: after reading 27; of word meanings 27
displays 48, 51, 54
distractions, minimising 44
drama: as aid to comprehension 38; to convey moods 63
DVDs 47, 90

EAL (English as an Additional Language), student difficulties 64
EAL (English as an Additional Language) texts: and motivation 46–7; for reading practice 24; withdrawal lessons 89
emphasis, and meaning 24
encouragement 24–5
enjoyment 47, 91
errors, ignoring 25
evaluation, of information from texts 37
examination instructions, comprehension of 41
examinations, practice for 41
EXIT (Extending Interactions with Text) 37
extracts, use of 47
eyesight problems 5–6, 92–3

family conversations, and vocabulary development 9
feedback: positive 25; from students 58
fiction: comprehension 34; for reading practice 23–4
finishing reading sessions, parents/carers advice sheet 77
Five finger test 30–1
flash cards 90
fluency, maintaining 26
form room reading 53–4; teacher advice sheet 88
formats, of reading material 48
foundations, of reading 45
frustration level 30
fun 47–8
fun activities, vocabulary development 62

games: for reading practice 23, 60, 70–1; subject-specific vocabulary 82–4; withdrawal lessons 90
Gardner, S. 39
general knowledge: and comprehension 34; lessons for 63–5; non-fiction reading 23, 31–2; and reading development 11; and reading speed 42; teacher advice sheet 80; teacher awareness of 63–4
genres 34
glossaries, use of 83
glue ear 4
grammatical conventions 34
graphic novels 24
group discussions, and vocabulary development 10
group reading 21
gum-chewing 43

habit, and reading speed 43
habits and techniques: reading lessons 55–8; slow readers 92
Hamman, P. 42
Hangman 71
Hasbrouck, J. 42
hearing loss 4–5
hobbies/interests sharing 53
home–school links 49–51
homes, as sources of material 53
homework 9, 41
homonyms 61–2

identification games 71
idioms 60–1
independent level 30
individuality, of students 21
information books, for reading practice 22–3
information, for parents/carers 49–51

information from texts 37
information processing 93
instructional level 30
instructions for use of equipment 51
interaction: with texts 37; and vocabulary development 8
interactive word banks 83
interest: loss of 45; and motivation 46, 48; and reading competence 29, 33
interest boxes 53
internet, research 61
Introduction to the Library sessions 51
IT: for reading practice 22; use of 41

joke books, for reading practice 23
Joke Days 90

keyword booklets 40
knowledge: activating 37, 64; and reading competence 29, 30
Kunzer, S. 39

language, explaining unfamiliar 31
language skills 6–7
languages, similarities 61
learning styles 13–14
library-based tasks 52
library books, donations 52
links, for libraries 52
Listening Books 90
longer texts, reading strategies 44

magazines: for reading practice 23; withdrawal lessons 90
mainstream lessons: active reading 33; comprehension development 33–41; extending vocabulary 40–1; fiction comprehension 34; non-fiction comprehension 35–9; non-fiction reading 31–3; overview 29; readability of texts 30–2; reading levels 29–31; reading speed 42–4
Manga 47, 90
matching words and meaning 82
maths vocabulary 84–5
medical problems 4–6
memory: assisting 37; auditory memory 15–16; and comprehension 35; and reading speed 42; subject-specific vocabulary 41; visual 14–15
mentors 19–21
mimicry 24–5
mishearing of words 7
misinterpretation of words 7
mnemonics 63, 70
modelling: good reading 24, 35–8; library use 52; reading speed 66
motivation: increasing 45–8; reader questions 19

names: clarifying 41; and vocabulary development 10
National Curriculum, and vocabulary development 8–9
National Literacy Association 12
National Literacy Trust 49–51
networks, for libraries 52
newspapers: for reading practice 23; use of 95; withdrawal lessons 90
noise, and vocabulary development 8

non-fiction: comprehension 35–9; for reading practice 22–3
non-fiction reading 31–3; active reading 33; for meaning 57–8; techniques 32–3; things to be aware of 32; use of diagrams 38; withdrawal lessons 90
note making 33, 37, 68

observation, of reading behaviour 18
'Odd Man Out' 70
old English 63
one-to-one reading practice 17
online resources, use of 10
organisations and associations 49

pair reading 21
parent/carer support 49–51
parental understanding, and vocabulary development 9
parents/carers: reading skills 19; reading to/with children 19–20; working 8
parents/carers advice sheets: encouraging reading 50–1; hearing children read 76–7; reading resources 79; reading with child 78
Parents' Evenings, library promotion 52
peer support, and vocabulary development 9
peer tutoring 19
Pelmanism 71
personal recommendations 48
phonetic irregularity 25
phonic knowledge, using 25
PHSE and study skills, teacher advice sheet 87
plays: and motivation 47; withdrawal lessons 89
poetry: and motivation 47; for reading practice 22
positive feedback 25
PQRS (Preview, Question, Read and Summarise) 33
prediction 27
prefixes 10, 62
print conventions 34
print size 44
promotions, school libraries 51, 52
prompting 25–6
proverbs 61
public libraries, links with 52
publishers' resources 40
purpose, of reading 35, 37, 42
puzzle books 23

questioning, while reading 35
questions: for clarification 28; to develop understanding 27–8; for slow readers 92–3
quiet corners 51
quiz books 23
quizzes 62; and vocabulary development 10, 71; vocabulary development 84

RAP (read, ask, put) 36
Rasinski, T. 42
readability: measuring 30–1; and reading age 29; of texts 30; worksheets 31
readathons 49
reader types, at secondary and college level 17–18
reading: as community action 49; purpose of 35, 37, 42
reading ages, variance 18
reading aloud: and motivation 46; parents/carers advice sheet 76–7; and reading speed 43; timing 27
Reading Assemblies 54

reading behaviour, observing and recording 18
reading challenges 51
reading competence, factors affecting 29
reading events 48–9
reading for meaning, parents/carers advice sheet 76
reading for understanding 67
reading groups 48, 51
reading lessons: comprehension 67–9; general knowledge 63–5; habits and techniques 55–8; overview 55; reading speed 65–7; self-evaluation 55–6; subject-specific vocabulary 69–71; techniques 56–7; visualisation 68–9; vocabulary 58–63
reading levels, Betts' typology 30
reading matter, students' choice of 22
reading mentors 19–21
Reading Newsletters 19–20
reading practice 17
reading programmes 90
reading promotion 54
reading questionnaires 18–19, 55–6
reading resources, parents/carers advice sheet 79
reading speed: developing 42–4; lessons for 65–7; measuring 66; modelling strategies 66; reader questions 19; slow readers 42–3
reading techniques 56–7
reading to children, parents/carers 78
reading with child, parents/carers advice sheet 78
recommendations 53
reconstruction 39
recording: information from texts 37; interesting words 54; of reading behaviour 18
reference books: games with 61, 62–3; for reading practice 23; use of 10, 54
regular practice, for reading speed 44
relationships between words, and vocabulary development 10
resources 22–4, 48; fiction 23–4; IT 22; non-fiction 22–3; poetry 22; scripts 22; song lyrics 22; students' choice of 22; subtitles 22; withdrawal lessons 89–90
responding, parents/carers advice sheet 76
restricted vocabulary 7–10
restructuring 39
reviewing, before reading 32–3
rewards for reading 54
rhyme, recognition of 7
Riddle Weeks/Days 90

scaffolds 35–8; EXIT (Extending Interactions with Text) 37
scanning 32–3, 56
scene setting 26–7
school libraries 51–4
scripts, for reading practice 22
secondary level readers, types 17–18
self-evaluation 55–6
self-questioning 35, 37
sequencing tasks 39
short courses 46
short stories: and motivation 47; for reading practice 24; withdrawal lessons 90
silent speech 43
skill development 18
skimming 32, 42, 56
slow readers 42–3; teacher advice sheet 92–3; *see also* reading speed

Index

SMOG assessment 30
solitary play, and vocabulary development 9
song lyrics, for reading practice 22
sounding words out 26
sounds, awareness of 7
Speech and Drama qualifications 91
Speech and Language therapy services 7
speech patterns, awareness of 7
speed of reading *see* reading speed; slow readers
spoken language, importance to reading 6–7
SQ3R (Survey, Question, Read, Recall, Review) 33, 38, 68
story telling sessions 52
storylines, commonalities 28
strategies: appropriate 37; encouraging 24–5; for prompting 25–6; reading speed 66; for unknown words 18
strategy guides, for reading practice 23
student advice sheets: comprehension 94; reading for note taking 68; reading speed 66–7; vocabulary development 63
student book groups 48, 51
student interests, and motivation 48
student librarians 51
student motivation, increasing 45–8
students: individuality 21; as sources of material 53
sub-vocalising 43
subject-specific vocabulary: lessons for 69–71; teacher advice sheet 82–6
Subject Ten Questions 82
subtitles 22
suffixes 10, 62
summarising 28, 36
support strategies: attention problems 11–12; auditory memory 15–16; comprehension 35–9; comprehension development 26–8; extending vocabulary 40–1; hearing loss 5; language skills 7; motivation 46; reading speed 43–4; visual memory 14–15; visual problems 5–6; vocabulary development 10; withdrawal lessons 91; worksheet readability 31
surveys 52
Swap Boxes 54
syllabification 26
synonyms 10, 61
synthetic phonics 13

Taboo 71
talking about books 53
talking with children, parents/carers advice sheet 76
teacher advice sheets: active reading 81; assessment of vocabulary and general knowledge 80; form room reading 88; PHSE and study skills 87; slow readers 92–3; subject-specific vocabulary 82–6; withdrawal lessons 89–91
teachers: awareness of student difficulties 35; knowledge of students 63–4; library recommendations 52
teaching methods 13–14
teaching strategies, vocabulary 63
techniques and habits, reading lessons 55–8
techniques, and reading speed 43
television: and motivation 48; and vocabulary development 8
text: grammatical conventions 34; varying size 44
text marking 39

text-to-diagram activities 38, 68
texts: construction 35; genres 34; interacting with 37; and motivation 46–7; readability 30; reading strategies 44
The Teaching and Learning Toolkit 19
theatre trips 24, 47, 49
thesauruses 61, 62–3; for reading practice 23; use of 10, 54
timers, use of 27
Tindal, G.A. 42
top-down teaching 13, 14
tracking 43, 91
trading cards, for reading practice 23
training, for mentors 20
'Twenty Questions' 70
types of readers, at secondary and college level 17–18

undiagnosed medical problems 4–6
unknown words, strategies for 18

variety, and motivation 46, 47–8
verbal interaction, and vocabulary development 8
visual memory 14–15
visual problems 5–6, 92–3
visualisation 27, 38–9, 68–9
vocabulary: acquisition 9–10; adequacy 34; classifying words 59; examination instructions 41; extending 40–1; fun activities 62; lessons for 58–63; maths 84–5; and reading speed 42; restricted 7–10; revision 41; subject-specific 69–71, 82–6; teacher advice sheet 80; teaching 9–10; variations in 58
vocabulary lists 69–70
vocabulary resources 40
volunteer mentors 20–1

websites 47, 54
Whitebread, D. 12
Who/What/Where am I? 83
whole class activities, vocabulary development 71
whole school events: form room reading 53–4; holding events 48–9; home–school links 49–51; overview 45; promoting reading 54; school libraries 51–3; student motivation 45–8
withdrawal lessons: overview 17; resources 89–90; teacher advice sheet 91
Word a Day/Week 54
word banks 83
word games 60, 70–1
word grouping 44
word lists 69–70, 84
Word Loops 71, 84
word maps 10, 40
word meanings, discussing 27
word play 8
word quizzes 10
word recognition, and reading speed 42
word relationships, and vocabulary development 10
word searches 82
word webs 70
words: mishearing/misinterpretation 7; origins 61, 63
working parents, and vocabulary development 8
worksheets, readability 31
World Book Day 49

year group events, school libraries 51

Printed in Great Britain
by Amazon